C000146111

An Ever-Rolling Stream

This book is being sold in aid of the
Chengelo Educational Trust (UK), of which
Norman Wyatt is the Honorary Secretary and
Dr. Peter Green, Director of the Diocese of Durham's
Lesotho Project, is the Chairman.

The C.E.T. exists to support Zambia's
CHENGELO SECONDARY SCHOOL,
which serves the needs of both native Zambians
and the children of ex patriates.

The school was founded in 1988 by
Russell Wyatt and two other farmers
in the Mkushi area of Zambia, and currently has
two hundred and fifty boarding pupils.
The curriculum leads to the International G.C.S.E.
Russell Wyatt is Chairman of the
Governing Body in Zambia.

An Ever-Rolling Stream

by

Norman Wyatt

Illustrations by **Charles Bone**

Time, like an ever-rolling stream,
Bears all its sons away;
They fly forgotten, as a dream
Dies at the opening day.

SMH BOOKS

British Library Cataloguing in Publication Data
A catalogue record for this book is available from the
British Library

ISBN 0 9512619 3 2

© Norman Wyatt

All rights reserved. No part of this publication
may be reproduced, stored in a retrieval system,
or transmitted in any form or by any means, electronic,
mechanical, photocopying, recording, or otherwise,
without the prior permission of the publisher.

First published November, 1993 by
SMH BOOKS
Pear Tree Cottage, Watersfield, Pulborough,
West Sussex, RH20 1NG

Typeset by
Maggi - The Business Centre, Pulborough

Printed and bound in Great Britain by
Biddles Limited, Guildford, Surrey

to Max

Acknowledgements

Thanks to my brother Paul, who first gave me the idea of writing down my memories — by writing down his own; to Paul and Russell, for their written criticisms of the first draft of my chapter on Dad and Grandpa Wyatt;

to Mary, for putting me straight about Grandma Norman; also to Ruth and Janet, for their criticism that the first draft had no character sketches of women in it (I apologise to them in advance for the word picture of Mrs. Davis in the book, and I expect I shall hear further from them!);

to Kath Hartley, in whose house I started to write this book, and who berated me for the paucity of what I wrote first about Max, and

finally, to Sandra Saer, who made me re-write the first chapter several times, and whose gentle bullying helped me to improve the text greatly.

N.W.
Summer, 1993

CONTENTS

Introduction

The pages which follow sketch the outline of a lovely and lively man who seems to have grown younger with the passing of the years. All human beings are worth listening to, many are interesting, and a few are fascinating. Here is the outline of one such; he writes with humour and insight, courteously revealing his pilgrimage so we can journey with him, walking but never growing faint.

I did not know Norman Wyatt until he was of mature years but of adventurous spirit. I am delighted with this fuller account of how he has come to be what he is — one who invites us to share his personal adventures with him.

Michael Guildford

Chapter 1

Setting the Scene

I have always been told that it is a mistake to return to the scenes of one's childhood after a long absence. I am not sure that this is true. Certainly one should not go unless prepared for a profound emotional experience. On a lovely late summer day in 1992, I re-visited the Sussex village of Walberton with Max, my wife, and my second brother Russell, on holiday from his home in Zambia. We went to see Pigeon House Farm, which was our family home from 1923, when my parents arrived bringing me as a toddler of two and my brother Paul, a babe in arms, until 1958, when the last of us left the village.

There must have been some unusually powerful magic in the air that day. Although I have been back at odd times since 1958, never before have I been so moved by the experience as I was then. The air seemed full of voices long since silenced. Forgotten incidents leapt to mind, powerfully reinforcing oft-remembered ones. Familiar faces I have not seen for many years looked at me in familiar places — and vanished. A strong desire to record something of them came over me ...

Walberton lies some five miles from the English Channel on the one side and two or three miles from the South Downs, on the other. The main road from Chichester to Arundel runs along the northern edge of the Parish, away from the village itself. Thus, unlike many Sussex villages, it is largely free from passing traffic. The Doomsday Book called it 'Walburgstone'. It also recorded that the village had 'wood for four hogs', which piece of otherwise useless information was used by the bullies at Grammar School to torment Paul and me — my parents being the other two hogs.

The Walberton I knew was an unremarkable village, the older houses being of flint and thatch, the rest a hotch-potch of late Victorian, Edwardian and pre-war houses and bungalows of the less expensive type. It was a post-feudal village, with no Lord of the Manor, though it did boast a Georgian mansion occupied by the remnants of a decaying old 'county' family.

As well as several smallholdings, there was one larger farm which belonged to my maternal grandfather, although he never farmed it. My father became his tenant in 1923 and bought the farm thirteen years later, with its new house, three cottages and extensive buildings for the princely sum of £6,500.

The village also had all the usual standard features — an ancient Parish Church, an austere Victorian Baptist Chapel, a school, a pub, a pond, a green, and a playing field.

It also had a rigid class structure, disregarded at one's peril. Children of our class did Not, repeat Not, play with the children from the Council Houses. My Mother explained that they were rough and did not have good manners. We might learn to speak in the way they did, using the south-coast glottal-stop in words like 'butter' or 'better', and thereby debar ourselves from a place in polite society. On the other hand, we were taught in a rather subtle way to despise the 'officer and county' class folk, of whom there were a few in the village.

The exaggerated hot-potato-in-the-mouth way of speaking which was used by such folk in pre-war days, was often the subject of hilarious ridicule around our table. It now seems extraordinary that anyone ever spoke like that, and the dialogue in some of the earlier war films still sends us into convulsions of laughter.

Broadly speaking, the upper class and the working class went to the Parish Church — if they went anywhere. The middle class went to Chapel — and that included us. It also included the large Butcher, Grocer, and Draper family in the village, the Engineering family and some of the smallholders.

In the 'twenties and 'thirties, life and attitudes were so different to those prevailing today that, even as I write, I wonder if I am caricaturing them. But I think not. Not only were the social dividing lines strict and observed by all, but also the religious and cultural ones. Some of them survived the upheavals of the Second World War and lingered on until I left the village in the late 'fifties. For example, I have never set foot inside the village pub to this day. If I had ever done so, it would certainly have been seen by someone and would have caused deep concern for my soul among my Chapel friends. Also, I had never been inside the Parish Church until my father's funeral on a bitter January day in 1945. Even then, we had to obtain special dispensation from the Bishop of Chichester for the Service to be held there.

My father died at the full peak of his manhood, at the age of fifty-two. He was known far and wide, so there would have been no possibility of getting even half of those who wanted to attend, into the Chapel. In these ecumenical days, it is hard to believe that the Baptist/Brethren Elders who conducted that Service would not even let the Parish Priest say the Benediction in his own church! I was sent by my mother to tell him so, and I still cringe at the thought of it, after almost fifty years.

based on ignorance, there was in those days a sense of honour and duty in human relationships so largely lacking today. Now the prevailing thought is to stand up for one's rights; then, it was to do one's duty, regardless of the consequences.

The world of my youth was also peopled by marvellous characters, several of whom are described in this book. One of them was John Smith, a staunch Chapel man. After he reached seventy, he used to say 'I'm only a trespasser in this world! I've had my three-score years and ten.'

Now I also am only a trespasser ...

On that late summer day we visited the old churchyard, where a score or more of the names which were once daily on my lips are now graven in stone. Other men, whom I knew as well or even better, also lie there within a few yards of my father and grandfather. As I have sought to recall those thirty-five years of my life spent in Walberton, it is the memory of these men that comes back most powerfully. For the moment they are lost to me, and Gray's Elegy is so true —

> *The breezy call of incense breathing morn,*
> *The swallow twittering from the straw built shed,*
> *The cock's shrill clarion, or the echoing horn,*
> *No more shall rouse them from their lowly bed.*

I know in my heart that this is not all that there is to be said. In Christian hope, I await that other world where, to quote St. Paul, 'This corruptible will have put on incorruption, and this mortal will have put on immortality'. From this standpoint I write these pages.

Chapter 2

Dad and Grandpa Wyatt

As a lad in my early 'teens, my father sent me on my bike to Barnham, two miles away, to take a message to his father, who was known to all the world as Grandpa Wyatt. I arrived as Grandpa and Grandma were having their daily Morning Prayers.

I stood waiting in the hall of their house listening, round the half-open sitting room door, to Grandpa's voice as it went on and on in *extempore* prayer. The Westminster chimes of their mantlepiece clock sounded the quarter, then the half hour. Still he went on in devout prayer and praise. All the bad things he came to were attributed to the Devil, whose defeat he implored. All the good things were recorded too, as matters for praise and adoration. The clock chimed the three-quarters, but still there was more, much more. Eventually my grandmother fidgeted, which was a sign that practical things needed attention, and the prayer was rounded off in suitable words. That was my grandfather, and that was his daily practice. What Macaulay wrote of the Puritans was true of him: 'The physical world about them was only a pale shadow of that inner spiritual world in which they lived'.

My father died three years before his father. It surprises me even as I do it, that I can write about them together. There was a strong feud between the two of them, and naturally, I took my father's side. It is now forty-four years since Grandpa was found by my aunt Beckie sitting up in bed with his open Bible on his knees, but gone to be with the Lord whom he had served with unswerving devotion all his life. Their earthly remains lie side by side on land once farmed by my father, now part of Walberton Churchyard.

Grandpa Wyatt

As I look back at them, over the expanse of nearly the whole of my adult life, I realize *how alike* they were. Both were huge men, big in every way. Grandpa with his twinkling blue eyes, his ginger beard, and clad in his Norfolk jacket and knee breeches. Dad, dark with his Scottish mother's hair, and his enormous farmer's leather jacket with the poacher's pocket, in which on cold days on the farm, his little Jack Russell terrier sat. They were men of a type that has all but disappeared under the levelling roller of our plastic and electronic civilization. They were men of uncontrolled emotions. Tempers flared easily, tears came readily, and so did laughter. The world they lived in was vivid with Biblical imagery, for they lived every moment of every day in the power of its poetry. They would not have called it poetry, for every line, every jot and every tittle of it was to them God's truth.

Apart from their knowledge of the Bible, which they invariably called 'God's Word', they were almost completely uneducated. Grandpa left school at the age of twelve; my father was not much older when he left. (I was taken from school at fifteen before I had a chance to sit for matriculation but, more important, before the evils of a worldly education had corrupted my mind too much.) I am not mocking them; I owe them far too much for that.

Above all I owe to them the conviction which I have had for over fifty years without a moment's doubt — that God IS, that God is the pure Light of Holiness, that God loves me, that he loves all the world, that this is the bedrock of life, and the touchstone to which everything else must be brought.

Nevertheless, it has taken me many years and much torture of soul to overcome the extreme fundamentalism which distorted their world view. Fundamentalism has the power to load its devotees with an enormous feeling of guilt, should they deviate so much as a hair's breadth from its tenets. Many a time in my youth, Grandpa Wyatt laid his powerful hands on my shoulders and looking, it seemed, into my very soul said, 'My boy, the Devil is trying so hard to deceive you!' Whatever other virtues they may have, none of my confessors or mentors of recent years have shown a hundredth part of the concern for my soul that Grandpa and Dad always showed.

Grandpa was like nothing so much as an Old Testament Prophet. He could read such passages as those about the slaughter of the Amalekites — 'The Lord will have war with Amalek from generation to generation', without a qualm or a word of explanation. It made one's hair stand on end to hear him read from the Psalms that 'the wicked shall be turned into hell and all the nations that forget God'. But the tears would run down his face as he read it, and as he pleaded with the congregation to 'get right with God'.

Nor were these things kept in the realm of theory alone. When the crackling wireless set spilled out the news that Edward the Eighth had abandoned the throne of Empire for the bed of an American divorcee, out came the words of the Book of Proverbs: 'The heart of a wise man is in his right hand, the heart of a fool is in his left'. When war came, he would have meted out not only to Hitler, but to the entire German race, the fate decreed for Amalek, and not left them man, woman, child, ox, sheep or ass alive, and he said so on every possible occasion.

Both Grandpa Wyatt and my father found within the pages of their beloved Bibles everything they needed to accommodate their mercurial temperaments. They were at home with the barbarities of Joshua, of Judges and of David's early life. The triumphs of the Chosen People of God were identified, of course, in their minds with the rise of the British Empire. In their moments of defeat, they could rail against God like any Psalmist but it always ended, like the Psalms, in words of patient submission. They also rose in exaltation with Isaiah, or borrowed Job's language in their frequent depressions. The Book of Revelation and the Apocalyptic parts of the Gospels were the basis of many of their weekly sermons in the Chapels and Brethren Assemblies of the area. Yet they also entered deeply into the sufferings of Christ, and all the redeeming and transforming power of the Gospel.

I feel sad that I cannot sit with them and quietly tell them that I now see in their beloved Bible, the history of man's search for a true understanding of the mystery of God as well as of God's unfolding revelation of Himself to man; that there were great spirits who grasped a greater truth in every age, and that slowly, oh so slowly, men came to see that He was not some barbaric tribal god grinding his enemies to powder. Eventually they came to see Him incarnate in a tortured figure dying on just such a stake as their forefathers would have prescribed for their enemies in His Name. And last but not least, I recognize the Bible to be the faithful record of this long march of the soul of man.

In their lifetimes they would not have heard me out. Grandpa's anger with me would have been terrible. Dad would have been deeply hurt. Yet now they have been 'in the glory' for many years and they see no longer 'as through a glass darkly'. Not only will they have realized this but they will have much to teach this trespasser, when he rejoins them in a few years' time.

But there was more to them than all this. Grandpa was a romantic. The best thing he ever did was to marry my grandmother, a dark-haired and beautiful Scot. With enormous courage and faithfulness she loved and endured him for over fifty years, bore him nine children and died two years before him. She imparted her Scottish shrewdness to my father, which was the main difference between him and Grandpa Wyatt. Grandpa's wild unpracticality placed a great burden on Grandma Wyatt. Dad, with his kindly and sensitive nature, was quick to see this as a boy. He not only stood up for his mother, he helped her in every way he could to cope with providing for the daily needs of her large family.

When he grew up, my father was as successful in business as Grandpa had been unsuccessful. He went from strength to strength, all through the long depression of the 'thirties by sheer guts, very hard work and canny shrewdness. Grandpa, who attributed everything to the Lord, could not understand why the Lord had not prospered him as he prospered his eldest son. This was the basis of their feud, which lay deep but, largely because of my father's kindly spirit, seldom surfaced to spoil the family unity.

Both men loved good food — their tables groaned with it. Often the cups and plates rattled as they thumped the table in uproarious laughter. They loved and were adored by children; they loved farming and outdoor sports, and had wide circles of friends. My father's sudden death was a cataclysmic event in the community of which he was a central pillar. I am glad I was with him when he died. His last words were 'Keep Calm, Keep Calm!' In a way they were an insight into the lifelong struggle he had had with himself. I shall always be grateful, too, that I had the privilege of driving my grandfather round some of the scenes of his earlier years on the Downs near Lewes, a few weeks before the release he daily prayed for came to him. His last counsel to me was 'God has given you a gift, my boy. Use it!' The extent to which I have been able to 'keep calm' and 'use my gift' in an age with which neither of them would have had much sympathy, I owe more to their example and their prayers than to any other factor.

Perhaps in this neglected spot is laid
Some heart once pregnant with celestial fire;
Hands that the rod of empire might have swayed
Or waked to ecstasy the living lyre.

Grandpa Norman

Chapter 3

The Normans

The Normans were different. There is no disguising the fact that they were a cut above the Wyatts, and knew it. Not that my Grandfather Norman would have ever conveyed it by the slightest word or gesture. He had impeccable manners. As always in such matters, it was the women who conveyed it, and especially one family of girl cousins. But we will draw a veil over that. It was long ago, and we have long since outgrown our childish prejudices and grudges and learnt to respect each other.

Nevertheless, the rowdy parties which were frequently held in their home were occasions of exquisite horror to my brother Paul, my sister Mary, and me. We were made to feel ourselves the clod-hoppers we undoubtedly were in their eyes. My parents also disliked these parties, but for an entirely different reason. Not to put too fine a point on it, to them, the Normans were also 'worldly'. Strangely, it was my mother, whose relations they were, who held this view most strongly. But she was like all new converts to a minority view: her understanding of the point at issue was often in inverse proportion to her zeal.

To say that my grandfather Norman was totally worldly would be to do him a grave injustice. Like so many men of his era, he was an upright and honest man who feared God and honoured the King. Although he was devout in his religious duties, in no way did he, or could he have inhabited that glorious and sometimes terrifying world of the spirit in which my father and Grandpa Wyatt lived. He was a handsome man with a quiet patrician air. He moved with an easy grace in any society. By a series of judicious land transactions, he had raised himself from being a working farmer long before I came on the scene. He lived the life of what was then known as a 'gentleman'.

My very first memory of him is that of being lifted by my father to join him on the saddle of his immaculately groomed white horse, and trotting down to his home, 'Bentworth' in Barnham, where he lived in considerable style. Horse riding was not then the sole prerogative of teenage girls. 'Gentlemen' still rode on horse-back about the countryside in preference to riding in smelly and unreliable motor cars with their frequent punctures and thirsty tanks.

Like many another farming family from the hilly little villages of the West Country, among them the Langmeads, the Wills's, the Vinnicombes and the Crosses, William Norman had come up with his brothers to find farms in the broad acres of Sussex during the first decade of this century. He did not settle to the buying and selling of cattle as many of them did, but to the buying and selling of land. This he did with considerable financial success, acquiring in the process those airs and graces which went with his new-found status.

He not only sold farms, he lent the buyers the money with which to buy and farm them. Soon he had gathered in his train a number of struggling men, who were beholden to him for the very roofs over their heads and the food upon their tables. He took a keen interest in every aspect of their welfare. Conversations with him always began with polite but sincere inquiries after the well-being of the wife and all the children, whose names he always knew, for he had an amazing memory. He also had the strange gift in conversation of being able to bring any of them vividly to mind in just a phrase.

There was a certain Mr. Christmas whom Grandpa could recall most vividly. He would pull in his cheeks to simulate Mr. Christmas's gaunt features and in a whining voice say 'Poor little Christmas'. And there Christmas was in imagination, standing before you in all his simpering misery!

Grandpa loved to be the centre of attention and to make the grand gesture. Like the horse in the Book of Job, he 'smelt the battle afar off'. Invited or not, he would always turn up to every party or special occasion, and take the most prominent seat as of right. He always devised some new ritual to embellish the giving of the generous gift he brought to the birthday boy or girl, thus prolonging his time on centre-stage. And truth to tell, no family occasion would have been quite the same without his tall, dignified presence.

His three naughty daughters, of whom my mother was the second, mercilessly exploited him, knowing that for the sake of his reputation, he would honour their purchases made in his name. He did not know how to control them, and my mother was ill-prepared by his indulgence for her life as the wife of a working farmer.

Why have I not mentioned Grandma Norman? Alas, try how I may, I cannot recall her. I have only to shut my eyes to see my Grandma Wyatt and to hear her little chuckle. Grandma Norman died some years before her husband. He quickly married again so that he could continue to live in the manner to which he had become accustomed. He never showed a sign of deep affection for his new wife, any more than he had for Grandma Norman.

Grandpa was most at home in the world of men. Like the Pharisees of old, I sadly fear, he loved 'Greetings in the Market Places and the Chief Seats in the Synagogues'. Grandpa Wyatt would mutter darkly from the Psalms about 'Men of this world, who have their portion in this life'. But I am sure he would have loved a little of Grandpa Norman's success. I was one of Grandpa Norman's Executors and Trustees after his death. What was a fortune in the 'thirties and 'forties is peanuts today.

I passed 'Bentworth', recently. It was derelict amid a

garden of weeds. Before he died, he wept to my father that he had spent too much time in the affairs of this world and had neglected eternal things. He does not lie in that churchyard in Walberton. Somehow it would have been inappropriate for him to be buried there. He belonged to a wider and yet a far narrower scene. Poor little Grandpa! But I loved him and I honour his memory.

> *The boast of heraldry, the pomp of power,*
> *And all that beauty, all that wealth e'er gave,*
> *Awaits alike the inevitable hour —*
> *The path of glory leads but to the grave.*

Chapter 4

School

At the age of six I was marched down to the Village School by my mother and registered in the infants' class. My mother was resentful, and this conveyed itself to me. I started school life on the wrong foot and continued to be out of step with the organised educational world until, to my intense relief, I was removed from grammar school by my father at the age of fifteen. My mother wanted me to go to a private school, of which there were a number around. But at this time family finances did not even rise to the meagre termly sum that would have made this possible. My father was then only a few years into his long financial struggle.

None of this meant anything to a six-year-old. The only message the family tension conveyed to me was that school was a pain that I must endure as a duty, and in every way inferior to the wonderful world of the farm.

Thus it was that I eyed the Village School Mistress, Mrs. Davis, sourly. The dislike was instant and mutual. I had never before encountered hostility in an adult. She towered above me, huge and terrible as 'an army with banners'. From that moment, I got it into my small head that teachers, as a kind, were like Mrs. Davis. To this day I find myself instinctively withdrawing my right hand at the thought of her. I can still feel the sting of her wooden ruler on my knuckles. The hostile attitude I adopted towards all teachers from then on did nothing to smooth my path through my nine years of schooling.

I also looked on my classmates with contempt. They were the very children my mother had forbidden me to play with. 'THEY did not come from a farm, like me', I told myself, little snob that I had already become. Out in the playground I lorded it over them, imitating Mrs. Davis's behaviour in the classroom and became a holy terror myself. One of Mrs. Davis's sayings haunts me to this day, for my wife uses it to tease me sometimes, "Now children, you can go out to play, and Norman Wyatt don't choose all the games!'

Many years later, I discovered why Mrs. Davis treated me as she did. By that time I had long left school, and we were both members of the Parish Council. I found that she was an old-fashioned Socialist who thought that free school education was for the working classes only, and certainly not for the children of farmers. Some of our verbal encounters in Council Meetings did me no credit at all, and I am thoroughly ashamed of the way I sometimes spoke and acted towards one who was by this time a sad and bitter old lady. She had spent her life banging her head against the flint wall of the deep conservatism of rural Sussex, without making even the slightest impression on it.

This time, it was I who was in the Chair, and reputed to be the youngest Parish Council Chairman in England. That I was aggressive and self-opinionated was partly due to her teaching and example, but that does not in any way excuse me.

At the age of nine, I was transferred to grammar school at Chichester. There the Masters were even larger than Mrs. Davis, and much more terrifying in their black gowns and mortar boards. My very first encounter with one of them was when I was ordered to write my name on an exercise book. I was doing this somewhat laboriously when a loud voice said, 'Boy, put that pen in your other hand!' I replied 'But I am left-handed, Sir. I can't write with my right hand'. 'Don't be so impertinent, Boy!' was the reply, 'No one in this school is allowed to write with his left hand.' That was the spirit in which my life at Grammar School started, and it continued much in that vein.

What happened out of class was sometimes worse than

what happened in it. Paul and I had our fair share of bullying. In all fairness to the school, this mostly took place on the train for Barnham to Chichester where we were beyond the supervision of the Masters. It would never have come to light except that Paul could not explain to my parents the quite severe injury to his hand which he managed to keep hidden for some days after it happened. This was caused by the bullies slamming the train door on it. We had both already silently endured the punishments our parents gave us for our torn blazers and mutilated caps, also the work of these bullies.

I shall never forget the storm that this caused, for my father was a formidable character when roused. Masters and Headmasters and indeed 'all the host of heaven' held no fears for him once he was on the warpath. The bullies were found and thrashed by the head in front of the whole school. This episode did nothing to endear us to the school or the school to us. My father was not always a very rational man. As he quietened down, the resolve grew in him to remove me from the whole atmosphere as soon as possible.

*   *   *   *   *

As I look back over my life, in which I have had quite a lot to do with the educational world, I am amazed and delighted at the change for the better that has come over it. As British General Secretary of an international missionary society, a considerable part of my time was given to recruiting teachers for our various schools in southern Africa. Also, during my thirty-five years in the Gideon Movement, I visited a great many schools each year all over the British Isles, as well as in other parts of the world. I have been a Governor of one or two schools and these experiences have led me to admire and respect the teaching profession greatly.

I have also been extremely fortunate, on the various

occasions when I myself have been a candidate for some post, to have key people on the selection panel wise enough to know that there are other roads to the tree of knowledge apart from those provided by formal education.

Even in my own disastrous experience of school there were one or two teachers on whom I look back with affection. Among them was 'Fishy' Scales, my History master at grammar school. He was a charming man who assumed such an air of hurt astonishment if anyone should dare to misbehave in his class that we did not often do so. He was a brilliant teacher, and his enthusiasm for his subject was infectious. He imparted to me not only a great love of history, but of language too. He was a master of the rounded sentence, the memorable phrase and the subtly expressed idea. He would walk about the classroom repeating over and over some particular expression that had caught him in its magic. He would twist his gown round and round his arm, raise his hand high and rush towards the blackboard to write it down before it was forever lost. I used to relish some of these sayings and repeat them to myself, copying his mellow, gentlemanly voice, and imitating his gestures. He was in the grand tradition of English eccentrics. I never saw him, or heard anything about him after that great day when the edict came from my father that I would not be going back to school again. I have often wondered if the whole course of my life would have been quite different had some female version of 'Fishy' Scales been my teacher at Infants' School, instead of Mrs. Davis.

But well into my thirties, my only recurring nightmare was that I was back at school again, my ear being twisted by some towering master and the words 'Think, boy! Think!' being shouted into it. What a relief it was, then, to awake in the calm of the farmhouse bedroom and look out of the window to where the cows were grazing quietly in the meadows. Gratefully I would slip on my clothes and get down to the farm for the morning 'Orders'.

Chapter 5

The Pre-War Farm

I became conscious of the farm as soon as I was conscious of anything. But it was many years before I was able to analyze what it was my father was doing, and why he was different from many, if not most, other farmers. I just knew that we had milking cows, a flock of sheep which my father loved and tended himself, a great many pigs and field upon field of poultry houses filled with free-range hens. I also knew that, apart from the smallholdings in the village which also had no arable land, our farm was unlike others around where teams of horses or the noisy new-fangled tractors ploughed the land, and arable crops were grown. However unbearable school was, I knew that I only had to endure it until a quarter to four each day, and then I could escape to the peace and fascination of the farm. Homework hurriedly and badly done on the train going home would cause a row tomorrow — but today the farm beckoned!

Until war came and changed everything, my father was a grassland farmer. His cattle increased in numbers far beyond the carrying capacity of our farm, and as soon as we grew old enough, Paul and I took part in the annual droves of young cattle to farms which had grass to sell, and in their return in the autumn. There was no thought in those days of carrying herds of cattle by lorries. We walked our cattle everywhere, sometimes to farms as far as twenty miles away. Many an adventure we had, especially when we encountered one of the Foden Steam wagons belonging to Penfolds of Barnham. One toot on their steam whistles and the excitable young beasts were up the banks and away over some exasperated farmer's corn fields. It sometimes took hours to get them back, and the air was often blue with the abuse we received. But entertainments were simple in those days, and we eagerly looked forward to these cattle droves.

Meanwhile, the centre of the farming enterprise was the dairy herd. My father was one of the first to instal a milking machine. I never knew him milk once in all the years, and we employed a succession of families of milkers. One of these was the Palmer family. The member of that family that I remember most clearly was Chris, who followed his father as head cowman. This was the top job on the farm, and enjoyed the top pay of forty-two shillings and sixpence, the best cottage with a beautiful garden and the usual perks of free milk, firewood, manure for the garden and, among other things, the right to shoot rabbits.

Chris was a steady, patient man, married to a town girl who was a member of the Exclusive Brethren. This sect is not to be confused with the Open Brethren beloved by my father and Grandpa Wyatt. The 'Exclusives' would have nothing to do with any other Church or group of Christians, whereas many of the little Independent Baptist Chapels were only kept going by Preachers from the Open Brethren. However, to give the 'Exclusives' their due, it was through his wife that Chris came to be a simple believer, who loved nothing more than to converse about the Gospels as we milked our way through the sheds of cows of an evening. (Of course I should have been doing my school homework, but milking was much more interesting, and brought me one shilling an evening — very generous pay.)

Along with the simple truths of the Gospel, the 'Exclusives' managed to impart many of their strange notions to Chris. He did not always fully understand them. He was a wizard with the new-fangled wireless, and had a wide reputation for being able to repair those crackling instruments. This became a useful side-line for him. Unfortunately, the Brethren informed him that the wireless was 'of the Devil'. Chris was a pragmatist. As the Brethren were so opposed to the Devil and all his works, they must not know of his involvement with the wireless repair trade. So if a visit from them was expected, he would hide his own set and all to do with it in the cupboard. He saw nothing inconsistent in this. He liked a quiet life and did not want to give offence. One night as we finished our work he looked at his watch and said to me, 'Well, if I get a move on I shall be just in time to hear what the Devil has to say about the news'.

Pressure from the Exclusive Brethren upon him increased as time went on, and he became harassed and careworn. The Brethren made him take his children away from the Chapel Sunday School. They required him to take them each week to the Assembly of their sect in Bognor. This he could not afford to do, either in terms of time or money. Eventually, the strain of all this made his wife have a severe nervous breakdown. She was taken away to a Mental Hospital. Chris bowed to the Brethren Elders and left us to go and live nearer to Bognor, where their malign influence on him could be complete.

For me, it was an early lesson in the evil power of religious fundamentalism. My father shared my feelings of deep hurt about it all. It also made me realize that I was really more interested in the people who lived and worked on the farm than in the farm itself. One of the local Exclusive Elders had the misfortune to meet my father one day in the market shortly after this episode. In the space of a few minutes, he heard a few passages of Scripture from my father's lips which he had previously overlooked and which put the fear of God into him. Alas, the fear of his fellow-Elders proved greater than the fear of God and nothing came of this encounter.

Meanwhile I was absorbing my father's business philosophy without realising it. As with everything, this was strongly re-inforced by quotations from the Bible. When the east wind blew and we were reluctant to go out to our tasks, he would say, 'The sluggard shall not plough because of the cold. Therefore shall he beg in harvest and have nothing'. When he brought morning candles to Paul and me before the days of electricity in the village, he would always say, 'Arise and shine for thy light has come, and the glory of the Lord has risen upon thee'.

Above all, I learnt from him the shame of debt, and of buying things I could not pay for. This did not include bank loans, which were regarded as a way of buying opportunity. He looked upon the banks much as he looked upon the bulls on the farm — as dangerous necessities which had to be handled with great care. 'Never, never,' he would say, 'let the bank have a greater equity in your affairs than you have yourself. Never be beholden to the banks, or to any man, and always negotiate from strength and not from weakness'. 'Banks,' he would say, 'are good servants, but bad masters'. These maxims have guided me all my business life, and though I have often been taunted for my over caution, they have kept me out of trouble financially. This philosophy of his was not a selfish one. He was very generous to those in genuine need. For the lazy and the feckless, he had no sympathy. He often quoted the great Apostle's words, 'He who does not provide for his own (dependants) is worse than an infidel'. Another favourite of his was the injunction to 'mind your own business, and work with your own hands, so that you may be a liability to no one, and have enough to give to those in need'. (I paraphrase the Apostle's words as he also did.)

All the things he enjoined upon us boys, he did himself and prospered in the doing. He hated war, and would seldom talk about his experiences in the Gallipoli Campaign of the First World War. The raucous voice of Adolf Hitler as it waxed and waned on the unsteady wireless set, filled him with foreboding. Was what happened in his youth going to happen again just as his own sons became of military age?

It so happened that my father, Paul and I were in London on the autumn day in 1938 when Mr. Chamberlain returned from Munich waving that little piece of paper and declaring that 'Mr. Hitler' had signed it, saying that it was to be 'peace in our time'. We had been up to the Dairy Show at the old Agricultural Hall in Islington, which was destroyed a few years later by 'Mr. Hitler's' bombers. As we looked out of the bus windows through the London fog, people were half-heartedly digging trenches in the parks and filling sandbags as though they only half-believed him. How right they were! But other and more important matters concerned us. We had to catch the train home to do the evening milking.

Chapter 6

The Hacketts

There is a theory held by some historians that an ancient race, neither Celtic nor Teutonic, is interspersed among the main races which inhabit these islands. Its members are very taciturn, it is held. They do not mix or marry except among their own kind.

The Hacketts, who worked on the farm, were the one family I have met who made me think that there might be something in this theory. They were certainly quite unlike any other people I have ever known. They have all long since died. But when I first knew them, the family consisted of four bachelor brothers who lived with their unmarried sister, Amy.

Bill, Amos, Steve and Fred were the names of these erect, slow and swarthy men, who used ancient words like 'lucifers'

The Hacketts

for matches and who called a wasp a 'wops'. Their skins were dark from permanent exposure to the elements both in winter and in summer, and their teeth were black from chewing tobacco. They were a part of the farm, having been there for centuries before we were ever thought of — or so it seemed to a small boy who held them in great awe. I still feel that awe as I recall them.

Each day they gravely walked into the farmyard for the morning ritual of the giving of the day's orders, their wickerwork lunch baskets slung over their shoulders, and their stiff corduroys tied with leather thongs below the knees. Then, mostly without a word, each would solemnly turn and go off to the tasks which had been allotted to him. They were skilled in all the labourer's arts and crafts, and held in complete contempt the many enthusiastic volunteers who came to lend a hand at haymaking and harvest time.

It was to Fred, the youngest one, that the others looked for leadership. If Fred approved, all went well. If Fred did not approve, then everything started to go wrong and the whole rhythm of the work was lost. My father was often driven to distraction by their stubbornness and obstinacy, but he could not sack them. For one thing, they went with the farm. For another, they were the envy of every other farmer for miles around for their steady skill.

One of the problems for a 'Trespasser' in writing about pre-war farming is that few people born post-war will understand the terms used. If I say that the rickyard after harvest, with its rows of symmetrical ricks built by the Hackett brothers, each with a day's threshing in it, was a sight to behold, what mental picture will be conjured up? Or if I say that sugar beet when singled by the Hacketts, did not need much seconding, what will I have conveyed? The tall waggon-loads of hay which they had loaded, did not fall off on the rough journey to the elevator by the Dutch barn — will that be double Dutch to most readers? Maybe hedge-laying or ditching will convey something to the conservation-minded. But what if I say that sheaves stooked by the brothers would stand through the roughest summer storm? (To ask them to go and stand up stooks that had been done by unskilled labour and had fallen over, was to invite a torrent of abuse that would have made a sergeant-major blanch.)

The farm was the limit of their world. On summer evenings after work, they could be seen sitting in pairs like crows on some stile, or leaning over some gate on the farm, surveying the work they had done that day or were to do the next day.

When holidays for farm labourers became compulsory, somewhen in the mid-thirties, my father was legally obliged to make them take holidays, as the other men had done for years. One summer week, about mid-week, I asked Steve to do some task, as he seemed to be at a loose end. He retorted 'I'm serposed to be on me 'ollerdays this week'. He had come in to the farm each morning, and had just stood about watching his brothers until the boring 'ollerday' week had passed, and he could get back to the real business of life.

After I had grown up somewhat, and was no longer a whipper-snapper beneath their notice, they would occasionally let down the veil of silent secrecy behind which they lived and talk about their former lives. Conscription in the First World War had claimed Steve and Fred. These two men, who had never before been further than Chichester (7 miles away), found themselves on the Western Front.

Fred even took part in the occupation of Germany. There, one day, Fred was on guard outside a Railway station. He said: 'I was standin' there on guard when a bloke looks out of a winder with a rifle in 'is 'and. Bothered if he didn't fire at me. It didn't 'arf rattle on my ole tin 'at.' On the rare occasions that Fred told this story, it always conjured up for me the picture of Wellington's squares of redcoats standing solid and defiant on the battlefield of Waterloo.

Steve had words of advice for the 'townies' with whom he trained, and who complained about the kick of the rifles making their shoulders sore. The old man would relate with a mischievous chuckle that he used to tell them, 'Don't 'old the gun so close to yer shoulder, then it won't 'urt so much'. The almighty kick of a loosely held .303 rifle must have been nearly enough to dislocate a soft town shoulder!

They didn't ask much of life, and they certainly didn't get it. Steve, the eldest who had a war wound, didn't come in to work until 7.30 a.m. instead of the usual 6.30 a.m. He was paid twenty-six shillings a week. The other labourers got thirty-seven shillings and sixpence for a full week. They had a milk allowance, could shoot rabbits for the pot, have all the wood they needed, and they had a large garden which was always full of seasonal produce.

One very wet evening during harvest time, I was standing in the shelter of an open shed as the men were knocking off work. Fred went by, his boots squelching water as he walked. 'Goodnight Fred' I called out, but got no answer. A second try was no more successful. My third effort was very loud. Fred turned and said 'I ain't said nothing to nobody all day, and I ain't going to say nort now!'

It was remarkable how they mellowed in their later years, and their deep concern for their sister when she had a time in hospital was quite touching. They would climb awkwardly into our family car for me to drive them in to see her at visiting times. They completely re-decorated their cottage to welcome her on her return. When Steve died, Fred and Bill and Amy accepted help and comfort, and opened up in a way which would have been unthinkable even a few years before. By now they had lost much of their moroseness and had developed quite an affection for our family.

Fred even managed a laugh at my small son one day. I had told Fred to put some manure on the rhubarb. Richard said, 'Don't we usually have custard on rhubarb, Dad?' When I had a spell of illness just before I left the village, great was their concern. Fred stubbornly refused to accept his week's wages (by this time, far more than thirty-seven and sixpence) as a kind of parting gift. When he came to stutter his 'Goodbyes', we were able to shake hands for the first time in all the years I had known him. I don't know if a tear stood in his steely grey eyes as he gripped my hand. My head was turned away so that he might not see the tears in mine.

Not one of the tasks at which they were so adept is done by hand today, and the tools they used with such skill are only to be found in museums. They did not understand the verbal Gospel. If they could have been so articulate, they would probably have said that religion was only one more of those many devices by which the educated keep the uneducated under their thumb. But they did understand the love of God when they encountered it, and responded in the only way they knew. The 'mouldering heaps' under which they all lie, so close to my father and Grandpa Wyatt are certainly not marked by 'animated busts or storied urns'. There is not even a wooden graveyard peg with the name 'Hackett' on it. Yet they and their forebears were devoted to the farm over the flint wall from where they lie, as were no others.

Oft did the harvest to their sickle yield,
Their furrow oft the stubborn glebe has broke;
How jocund did they drive their team afield!
How bowed the woods beneath their sturdy stroke!

Let not Ambition mock their useful toil,
Their homely joys, their destiny obscure;
Nor Grandeur hear with a disdainful smile
The short and simple annals of the Poor.

Chapter 7

The Rude Forefathers

Within a stone's throw of my father and Grandpa Wyatt lie Edward Booker, the Smallholder, Bill Sergeant, the Engineer, and Henry Humphrey, the Butcher and Grocer. Each was an important figure in our local pre-war world.

As sure as the sun rose, Edward Booker could be seen each Monday morning riding with Pasha Baker, his carter, to Barnham Market, in the horse-drawn trap. Edward, a huge man, took up nearly all the room, and squeezed in beside him was Pasha, a scrawny little boy, named by his illiterate mother after some hero of the Colonial wars of the mid-nineteenth century. I can hear now the crackle of the gravel as the trap ground its way to Barnham down the rough lane bearing the two old men to their one eagerly anticipated outing of the week.

Bill Sergeant would stop his lathe at any time to deliver a lecture on the state of the world and the sad decline of the British Empire. He attributed the latter in equal measure to the Trade Unions, to there being no discipline in the home any more, and 'no fear of God before men's eyes'. He would make a part for any car on his lathe and despised 'fitters' who just took a part off the shelf and fitted it to a machine. He was a crusty old character, but nevertheless delighted to take the mickey out of me or any other dissolute youth who came his way. All the young were dissolute to him. I am glad he did not live to see most of his predictions about our beloved country come true.

But Henry Humphrey had, and always will have, a special place in my heart. He was the Superintendent of the local Independent Baptist Chapel. It was there that our family went each Sunday for the 11 a.m. Service and, as children also, to both Morning and Afternoon Sunday School. Mostly we had visiting preachers of varying standards and abilities, but sometimes Mr. Henry Humphrey would be the preacher himself. He was a genial soul, and the warmth of his personality and his deep devotion to the Lord made up for any lack of homiletic skill as he faithfully set forth the Word of God. I often wondered as a child why he had spells of weeping in his sermons. I now wonder if they were not tears of frustration because he could not put into words the glory that filled is soul. He need not have worried on that score for it shone from his face. But of course he would not have been any more aware of that than Moses was when he came down from the Mount of God with a glory upon him that dazzled the people of Israel.

Henry was also easy to mimic, and our Sunday lunchtimes were often enlivened by our efforts along this line. My father would roar with laughter and thump the table until the glasses rang. For example, every Sunday as Mr. Henry gave out the notices he would say, 'Will friends please place their freewill offerings in the box as they pass out'. Badly controlled sniggers would emanate with equal regularity from the Wyatt pew. We used to keep a score of how many repetitions of the word 'Friends' he would be able to get into the notices. It would go something like this: 'Friends, we are going on Wednesday to visit the friends at East Dean. So will all friends please be ready for the coach at such and such a time, and please tell any friends who are not here this morning so that they and their friends can come too.' Unlike so many of the prophets of old, Henry's sons, Don and George, did walk in his ways. His wife, known to us as 'Mrs. Henry' was also a great pillar of the Chapel. I owe more than I can say to her carefully prepared and interesting Sunday School lessons.

On weekdays Mr. Henry presided over a large emporium at the village-street end of the lane leading to our farm. (No one would have ever though of calling him 'Henry'.) It was a butchers-cum-grocers, with his brother's drapers shop next door. Just as Bill Sergeant was a real engineer, the Humphreys were real butchers. They slaughtered and cut up their own meat, and the shop was always packed with men sawing and hacking away, and huge sides of meat being carried hither and thither over the sawdust-covered floor. 'Chopper' Stevens and his son Alec, as well as Don, all worked away there to satisfy the customers who came from far and wide. In the middle of them all, quiet and serene amid all the noise was the reassuring presence of Henry Humphrey. He 'sat light' to it all, for like my father and Grandpa Wyatt, it was in the world of the Spirit that he really lived. His conversation and his letters were peppered with Biblical quotations, and his interest lay more in the Chapel than in his thriving business.

Through the doorway with the creaking floorboard was the grocery department, where George Humphrey and Fred Cheesman presided, and from which errand boys set forth on their bicycles with huge front baskets groaning with goodies. Together with the butchery side, Humphreys Stores was the supermarket for all the surrounding villages.

One day in the thirties, I stood with my father in Barnham Market amid a circle of my elders and betters. It was a 'butchers' market', where fatstock for slaughter were sold. Sometimes as many as one hundred and fifty bullocks from the fattening yards of local farms would come under the auctioneer's hammer. Butchers came from all over the South of England to buy their beef, lamb, pigs and poultry. It was one of the great events of the week for folk from miles around. Mr. Henry was there with us when word came that Don's wife had just given birth to triplets. Henry's face broke out into a sweat, out came his handkerchief, as he stood transfixed and gently muttering, 'Well I never! Well I never!' 'The triplets' quickly became an important part of the local scene. They all grew into fine and godly men. They are not 'trespassers' yet, but I believe that all three are grandfathers now.

I did not bury Henry or Don, but I buried Mrs. Henry, Mrs. Don, George and many years later his wife Mary. Also, on a cold winter's day I buried George and Mary's baby son, who died at birth — and all in that God's acre where my father and Grandpa Wyatt lie. I had not been able to train as a Minister in any College, but I was fast becoming one, notwithstanding all, and increasingly in demand for such occasions.

Beneath those rugged elms, that yew tree's shade,
Where heaves the turf in many a mouldering heap,
Each in his narrow cell forever laid,
The rude forefathers of the hamlet sleep.

Chapter 8

Old Tommy Dowling

When war came and the drive to increase the Country's arable acreage was upon us, my father had to take on more men with labouring skills. We needed an expert thatcher, for one thing. Tommy was such a man.

I remember clearly the first time I met him and was subjected to his extraordinary way of communicating. It was not that he spoke the south country dialect, but that with no preamble he would burst out with something from his own train of thought. Unless you could divine what that had been, all communication ended right there.

I quickly got on to his wave-length, but that first time, I wondered what sort of half-wit my father had engaged. He was thatching a huge straw rick by one of the cattle yards, the product of several days' threshing. He approached me in his wobbling gait as though he were negotiating the deck of a battleship in high seas, spat out his tobacco juice and said, 'Ah Boy, t'aint this side, 'tis the other side'. He was obviously agitated about it so I drew him on in conversation until eventually I tumbled to it that he was trying to tell me the ladder he was using was all right for the side he was thatching, but not long enough for the other side of the rick, as it was built high above the base of the stock yard.

Tommy was a lovable character, an old sailor who seemed to know every port that the British Navy visited in those days when it was second to none among the world's navies. He had also had years on the Argentine cattle boats, and knew many of the great cattle exporters and breeders of those days. He was fascinating to listen to, and became a great favourite with the many students who came in the summer months.

He always spoke in the same series of short staccato sentences, with no introduction, preceded by a huge, disgusting spit of tobacco juice. For example, 'Funny little yeller fellers they Japs be,' a pause, then: 'I didn't harf hit him one' a long pause, then: 'Yeah, you should've heard his teeth rattle, all up Commercial Road'. You could then press him as much as you liked to find out how he got involved in a fight with Japanese sailors in Portsmouth, but all to no avail. He would round off the encounter with something like, ''Course I don't really hold anything against 'em. You has to live and let live don't yer?'

Sometimes he would get on the brain the name of some person who had impressed him in his earlier life and would go round muttering it to himself. One such was a cattle breeder named 'Crawford Douglas'. He would work away at his thatching or hoeing, saying to himself the while, 'Yep. Crawford Douglas'. Pause, then 'Crawford Douglas' and so on and on, until it nearly drove one crazy.

He came to us from a farming family not far away who had a reputation for driving a bargain beyond all reason. What

Tommy Dowling

he said about these twin farming brothers has become part of the vocabulary of our family, as have many another of his observations. In this case, and once again without saying who he was talking about he burst out one day with, 'Yeah, Boy, they had a good hidin' when they was young!' 'What do you mean, Tommy?' 'Well their father caught 'um givin' things away. He gave 'um a good hidin' and they've never given anything away since.'

One of his sayings that is in constant use in our family to this day is, 'T'aint him, Boy, 'tis her!' — a saying with many and varied uses, and a good starter for a feminist argument.

But it was Tommy's ventures into Christian things which provided some of the most repeated tales about him. One day an Evangelist was earnestly talking to Tommy about the need for faith. 'That's right sir, that's what I always sez,' he burst out with. 'Now you take them there calves. If I didn't have no faith that they would grow, what good would it be for me to feed 'em?' Retreat of one puzzled and beaten Evangelist.

On another occasion, as we moved together up and down the rows of sugar beet with our singling hoes, the conversation turned to the Sunday Services, and to some sermon we had heard. Tommy spat. And then out it came: 'No, Boy, I can't preach. I've never had no hand in that. I can hoe, Boy, and I can build a rick, and I can thatch too, but I can't preach'. Long pause, then, 'Mind you I used to go to Church. Used to wear a badge and all!'

He was particularly fond of my brother Russell. Several years after the war, when Russell had gone to Northern Rhodesia, he was very excited at 'Morning Orders' time. 'Had a letter from Russell, Boy'. Pause for spitting, 'Yeah, had one of they from my mother when I was in Malta in the first world war'. No amount of coaxing got from him what he really meant.

Tommy had an invalid wife, of whom he was very fond.

One evening several years after the war, we were at work in the fields when the village policeman came striding out to see us. By this time his wife was in hospital in Chichester, and the message was that Tommy was urgently wanted by his wife's bedside. We stopped work, and I drove him in to see her. There was little he could do, and he was dismissed, but told to be in readiness should he be wanted in the night. I took him back to the farmhouse so that I could drive him in again if a call came in the night. He would not come into the house. 'No, Boy,' he said 'I'll stay here in the car. I'll just take off me boots and me braces. I'll be all right here.' At three a.m., the phone went and Mr. Dowling was wanted in Chichester. As we drove along in the quietness of the night, hoping to be in time for him to see his wife before she died, he said, 'Ah boy, I thinks I shall have a widow.' 'Yes Tommy?' 'Yep. One about fifty-five.' 'Will you, Tommy?' 'Yep. You sees 'em advertized in the paper, don't yer?' 'Really, Tommy?' Long pause, then, 'I wonder if Mr. Vinnicombe (the local Corn Merchant) would know of one?' The frail little Mrs. Dowling died, and not long after, as we were greasing up the Combine Harvester, Tommy spat. 'She's coming to see me Sunday, Boy.' 'Who is, Tommy?' 'A widow.' On Monday morning after Orders I said, 'How did you get on yesterday, Tommy?' 'No good, Boy! No good! She was forty-five. I wants one of fifty-five!'

Tommy did eventually find a widow to be his house-keeper — for that was all he wanted. But she didn't last long, and Tommy spent his last working years on his own.

He didn't come in to work one morning, so after breakfast Max and I went round to his bungalow in the car. We found he had collapsed, and had been on the floor all night. We took him back to the farmhouse, put him to bed and called the doctor who promptly arranged for an ambulance to take him to hospital in Chichester. Before the ambulance came, he kept saying to Max, 'What about my money?' She thought he was afraid he would not get his wages, and reassured him that he would be paid through his illness, which was our invariable custom with staff. 'No, no,' he said, 'the money in my house'. It transpired that he had money hidden all over his bungalow. I went there with the local Bobby later in the day, and we found several hundred pounds — a small fortune in those days, much of it in unopened wage packets going back over years. He had little use for money, seldom buying clothes or taking holidays, and he grew much of his food in his garden.

In hospital he became a popular character, and stories about him filtered back through Max's nursing friends. He quickly spotted how busy the nurses were, and would nip out of bed to bustle about and help wherever he could. He really was quite ill, and the doctor sternly told him that he must stay in bed. 'Wot, me stay in bed, Doctor, when we'm so short-'anded on the ward?' was his retort.

I persuaded him that he must make a will, or his only son might lose his father's hard earned savings. He made me his executor. His instructions to me proved impossible to translate into legal jargon . . . 'Don't let 'im 'ave it all at once, Boy. He'll waste it, see! Let 'im 'ave it in dribs and drabs!'

When the many wartime helpers came back to the farm for nostalgic visits, it was for Tommy Dowling that they always asked first. Several times in later life, I have been greeted in some unexpected place by a voice in my ear which turned out to be that of one of these wartime visitors saying, 'Yeah, Boy, I can hoe, Boy, and I can thatch a rick, too!' Or, 'If you sees a fool coming down the road, you must 'ave 'im, Boy!'

He was the same age as my father. But he was not laid in that God's acre until my father had been there for thirty years.

> *No further seek his merits to disclose,*
> *Or draw his frailties from their dread abode.*
> *There they alike in trembling hope repose*
> *Upon the bosom of his Father God.*

Chapter 9

Brothers and Sisters

At the time of my birth in 1921, my father was working on Grandpa Wyatt's farm at Falmer, near Lewes. I am the eldest of our family of six. By the time my youngest sister, Janet, came along in 1934, my father was a well established farmer in his own right. Before she was old enough to be concerned with such things, the German armies, which had marched into Austria in 1936 were well on with their programme of laying Europe to waste, and all life in these islands was overshadowed by the clouds of war. Indeed the whole of my teens and early twenties were lived under the shadow of Hitler, and I was twenty-four when the German armies finally surrendered to General Montgomery on Luneberg Heath.

What has this to do with our life as a family of brothers and sisters? A very great deal. We lived within five miles of the Channel coast and on routes which the German bombers took to London as well as to Southampton and Portsmouth. If the wind was in the east, the fighter squadrons from Tangmere took off over the farm. If it was in the west, the Fleet Air Arm planes from Ford did likewise. By the end of the war there was not a field on the farm which did not have either a bomb hole or a piece of crashed plane on it. It was these considerations, both seen and foreseen, which caused my parents to send the three youngest members of the family to boarding school — as they thought, away from it all. (It was soon to be discovered that nowhere on these islands was out of the range of the *Luftwaffe*.) This effectively split the family as well as giving the younger ones a much better education than the older ones.

The upshot of this was that we older three had a much

Brothers and Sisters

greater bond with my parents and with the farm than the younger ones. Not only were we on the scene earlier than they, but we stayed at home much longer, even allowing for the fact that Paul served for several years in the army. Age came into it as well. Janet spent many of her pre-school days toddling round after me or my father, according to who was doing the most appropriate job at the time. When kindergarten-time came for her in the village, I was sometimes mistaken for her father by the other children when I went to collect her from school.

A further dividing factor was that there was far more money to play with when the younger ones came along than in my parents' first years of struggle to establish themselves on the farming ladder.

None of this is a gripe on my part. But it does illustrate the difficult decisions that parents had to make in wartime, and how they often 'got it wrong', in spite of all their agonizing. As it turned out, I think I had the best of it, in that I had far more of my parents than any of the others did.

I can remember my mother in her younger days as a jolly person, full of fun. This was certainly not true of her from the late 'thirties on. I remember her chattering and giggling with her two sisters, all talking at once and jostling each other like a bunch of school girls. Gradually her personality changed, and a gloom settled on her which became blackest night when my father died suddenly, towards the end of the war. I was close to my mother in those years. I did not perceive the change in her at first, and as she became more gloomy, so did I. What was quick temper in my father became bad temper in me for a while.

My brother Paul, fifteen months my junior, was a plodder, but determined and quite single-minded. His great success in life as a farmer and breeder of pedigree cattle has been achieved by the same shrewd assessment of the options open to him that brought my father success.

Mary who is fifteen months younger than Paul had Grandma Wyatt's beautiful thick, dark, curly hair. The first time I saw an adult cry was when my mother had to cut it all off because she had caught eczema at the village school.

Mary was a gentle child and suffered much from Paul's and my teasing, though we loved her dearly and did not mean it unkindly. She came into her own in the war years, when she practically ran the farmhouse and did all the cooking as my mother did less and less. This was no mean task for in summer the house was full of students who had come to do their bit on the land for the war effort, and there could be up to half a dozen Canadian soldiers to supper, after their day in the harvest fields. Mary is one of those people who quietly gets on with things without fuss or ostentation and whose contribution is often not recognized until they disappear from the scene.

The younger three were almost like a second family. By the time they were old enough to remember things, a quite dramatic change in the family fortunes had taken place. Russell was the family charmer. He inherited much that was best in both his grandfathers. He had Grandpa Norman's easy grace, and Grandpa Wyatt's capacity for spiritual things. He was popular wherever he went and outshone us all in any company.

Grandpa and Grandma Wyatt's Golden Wedding party
at Crowshall, 9 May, 1942

The two younger girls were fighters, stoutly asserting their rights against their older brothers and sister. They could not have known, of course, that theirs was a text-book example of how the younger children in a large family are supposed to behave. Once they went to boarding school, we saw little of them until, poor souls, they had to live with Mother in the depths of her extravagant and endless grieving for Father. It is amazing that they were both so successful in their careers — Ruth as a missionary in Swaziland and headmistress of a large school, Janet, as a pioneer in the use of music to help those with learning difficulties, for which she was honoured by the

Queen. Unlike my other brothers and sisters, with whom I have had the easiest of relationships, I have had to fight hard to get to know Ruth and Janet in adult life. They became strangers to me in the confused days of the war and its long aftermath.

In any large family there are bound to be special relationships. In my case, mine is with Russell. He was just about to leave school when my father died. It left him in a special kind of limbo. I tried hard to integrate him into the farming business which suddenly fell into my lap to manage. By then we had three farms with three milking herds, and a considerable acreage of arable land. I was not old enough or experienced enough to give him the fatherly guidance he needed. So when a missionary friend, a contemporary of my father said, 'Why don't you send him out to my brother in Northern Rhodesia for a while', both Russell and I jumped at the idea. Russell's long career in what is now Zambia is a story in itself. He has become a kind of patriarch himself, with a dozen or more grandchildren, a large farming business, and he is Chairman of the Governors of a secondary school there, of which he was a Co-founder.

My brother Paul is a 'trespasser' now. When Russell was in England recently, we gathered at Paul's home to celebrate this 'Coming of age' of both Paul and his wife, Ruth. How proud my parents would have been of them all. Maybe they were permitted to look on from that other world which is hidden from us mortals until our time comes.

56

Chapter 10

Pulborough and the Phoney War

In the late 'thirties, the growth of my father's cattle herd, and the increasing difficulty in finding summer grazing for our young cattle on other farms within reasonable distance, led to his joining with Alfred Bowerman, one of his Open Brethren friends, in the purchase of a farm at Pulborough. Alfred took the arable land and the farmhouse, and my father took the grazing land and the cowsheds as well as the water meadows on the east side of the River Arun, including a famous old piece of land called 'Fowl Mead'. This meadow had a number of 'Lammastide' rights on it owned by various people who had inherited them, and which had been passed down from father to son since time immemorial. 'Lammastide' is on 1st August. It is an old Saxon Christian festival first mentioned in King Alfred's chronicles, in which the first loaf made of that year's corn was used for Mass, hence 'Loaf-Mass' or 'Lammas'. Lammas-rights holders could cut hay on their strips of land, but had to clear it off the land by Lammas day, when all and sundry could turn their cattle in to graze.

The land itself had long since been in private hands, but the Lammas rights remained. My father bought them all out. The documents showing these rights were extremely interesting, and I was sorry to part with them when I was involved in selling the land years later.

But there was a far older and quite unpredictable power which laid claim to the water meadows from time to time, and that was the River Arun itself. In those days before the extensive drainage work which was later carried out in the lower Arun valley, there could be a flash flood at any time, which turned the whole area into a lake deep enough for even

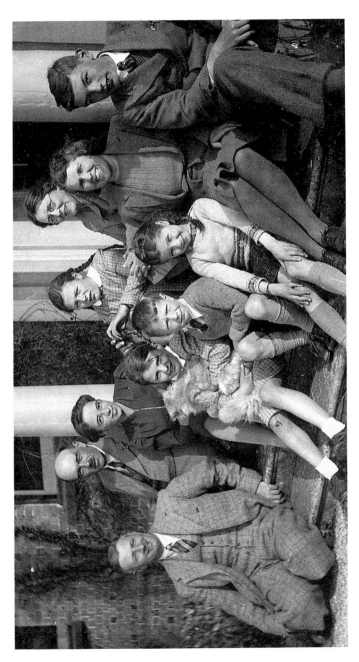

The Wyatt and Bowerman families at the Bowermans' house Courtwyke, Littlehampton. c. 1938

large cattle to have to swim to escape. Many a time when there was a period of summer rain, the 'phone would ring at Walberton to tell us to come post haste to get the cattle off. We had a boat for that purpose, but I do remember one occasion when I had to swim a section, for some reason I have forgotten. Maybe it was just youthful exuberance!

All these hazards were well worth enduring because of the amazing fertility of the meadows. The grass was unbelievably lush, and grew without abating, all the summer. The floods, which happened several times every winter were better than any fertilizer then available. It was a beautiful area, and I soon grew very attached to it and to the multitudes of wild fowl which either lived there or used it on their migratory journeys.

With the new farm came a dairy herd, which was milked by hand. My father employed two brothers to look after this herd: Sidney and Fred James. He also sent me up there

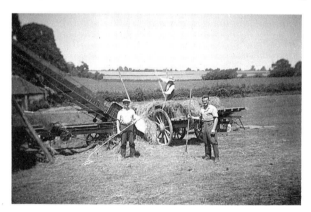

immediately after the outbreak of war, and I stayed there until the spring of 1940. That was the winter of the Phoney War. War had certainly been declared, but nothing happened! The popular idea had been that on the outbreak of war, the sky would be black with German planes, and we would all be gassed to death. We saw no planes that winter, and gas was never used during World War Two.

It seems now that Hitler spent the winter coming to terms with the fact that, contrary to his expectations, the Western democracies were prepared to fight, and that he would have to deal with them before getting on with his real aim of a *drang nach osten*[1] to destroy the Soviet Empire. There was certainly nothing phoney about the *blitzkrieg*[2] of Spring 1940 when it came. In a matter of weeks, France and the Low Countries fell, as well as half of Scandinavia. Our own expeditionary force came scuttling home on every imaginable floating thing, mostly without even their small arms. The war took to the air and the now famous 'Battle of Britain' began.

Right through the quiet winter of that phoney war, I was at Pulborough. My most vivid memories are of the people I met there. In Fred and Sidney James, I encountered for the first time an entirely different type of farmhand to the cussed old Sussex labourers I had been brought up with. They were from the West country. They were hard working, pleasant and companionable, as well as completely free from the wearisome old 'them and us' spirit that made relationships with local labourers so difficult.

But I also encountered in Mr. Bristow and his family, a stratum of society I had not met before. Mr. Bristow was a text-book example of that very English phenomenon, the 'gentleman's gentleman' — so brilliantly portrayed by P.G. Wodehouse. I had lodgings with the Bristows right through that long cold winter. Mr. Bristow was head gardener to the Rector of Wiggonholt. Every morning, dressed in his dark suit, polished boots, starched white collar and tie, his bowler hat firmly upon his head, he mounted his bicycle and went off to his day's work in the Rector's gardens. Although I was only a lad, he always called me 'Mr. Wyatt'. He had an

---

[1]   expansion to the east
[2]   lightning-war

old world charm and courtesy which came out in all his many
anecdotes, told through the steam of Mrs. Bristow's cooking as
we sat through the long and sumptuous meals she served in her
kitchen every evening.

Many of the stories had to do with the first world war. As
he talked of what 'Jerry' did or did not do, one felt he had a
polite and even affectionate regard for what we were, at that
time, all learning to call 'the enemy'. Certainly, as I look back
upon him over half a century, I
think he is one of the very few
men I have met in my life of
whom it could be said as it was
of Nathanael in the New
Testament, that he was 'a man
without guile'.

He loved to tell stories of his
employer, and not for the first
time I saw how the 'learned' are
regarded by men of little learning
but great wisdom. It appeared
that the Rector was puzzled and
frustrated by his own failure to
communicate with his
Parishioners. He sought Mr.

Mr. Bristow

Bristow's help. Mr. Bristow told
him that the way to win their hearts was to talk to them about
things they understood, like their gardens, their work on the
farms, or the wildlife which was all around them. But the
worthy cleric never could get it right. In the depths of winter,
when the ground had been iron-hard for weeks, he would ask
some man picking his brussel sprouts, how his carrots were
coming on. Or remark that it was good weather for
haymaking, when the sun came out feebly in June after a week
of rain.

Of course all this would be reported in the Pub that night

as further proof, if any were needed, that the Rector was a 'nutter'. The Rector himself could not understand why his overtures were met with scarcely suppressed mirth, and came to doubt the worth of Mr. Bristow's advice. Many of Mr. Bristow's stories were against himself, and he would laugh as heartily as any of us at his own humiliations, for even in those more courteous days, people were not lacking who delighted in humiliating those whom they considered unusual or inferior.

Dad Wyatt on the tractor during wartime

I was sad when my father called me back to the main farm somewhen in the spring of 1940. The six months living at Pulborough had been my first experience of living away from home and I had enjoyed it. But things were hotting up on the main farm as well as on the Western Front. It was to be the first summer of arable farming for us, with many new machines and techniques to master, and my father needed me.

While we were washing our hands for lunch in the garage of the farmhouse one June day, the wireless spilled out the news that on the orders of the French High Command, all resistance to the *Wehrmacht*[1] on the western front had ceased and France had capitulated to the Third Reich. It quite spoilt our lunch, and cast doubt for a few days on our hitherto unshakeable conviction that Britain could not be beaten in war.

---

[1]   German Armed Forces

Chapter 11

The War

The war is the one period of my life which I can remember in great detail. Every year, almost every month of every year stands out as though it were only yesterday. I was eighteen years old when Mr. Chamberlain made that famous speech which ended '... I have to tell you that no such undertaking has been received and that therefore this country is at war with Germany'.

Little did I know then that before it ended I would be married and my father would have died. What the war did to the world, it did to my life — it changed it forever.

As to many another of my age, the war came not as some great and heroic adventure, but as a confounded nuisance, and a much resented intrusion into my private world. These feelings were in no way ameliorated by the arrival of the army to take up residence in the two large establishments in the village — Avisford Park and Walberton House. Until 'D-Day' 1944, we were under an occupying army. If it had been the German army, it could hardly have been more resented than it was at first. The soldiers went where they liked and did what they liked all over our neat and tidy farm, without so much as a 'By your leave'. We were used to being the masters of our own territory, and we did not take kindly to being deprived of parts of it, and having defensive works erected here and there.

Further, it was my first experience of a large organisation which appeared to be run on totally irrational lines. For one thing the orders which were given to the men were not delivered in the calm and reasonable manner that was the daily morning practice on the farm. They were bellowed by men whose distorted faces made one wonder if they were not in the throes of an epileptic fit. When the soldiers came to do a job, such as digging a trench, three times the number needed came and got in each other's way. Often I thought that one of our labourers could have done the job being done by half a dozen, and in half the time.

Their officers were of the 'hot-potato-in-the-mouth' variety, and changed their minds about where they wanted their defensive aprons of barbed wire placed, every time the wind blew.

Their lorry drivers could perform the amazing feat of knocking both gate posts down when they drove through the farm gates! Apart from the seemingly pointless march, march, march up and down the village street, which they did with great gusto, they were about as useless a bunch of men as I have ever seen before or since.

Later on in the war, when I was a member of the Home Guard, I discussed all this one night with a First World War N.C.O. who was on guard duty with me. He explained that the old style Army catered only for one type of man — the 'bloody fool'. If you were not a 'B.F.' when you joined, the system was designed to quickly make you one. The idea behind it was to reduce you to a state in which you would instantly obey orders given by officers or N.C.O.s even though, in a rational frame of mind, you would realize that to obey meant certain death. This idiotic philosophy had to change if we were to stand any chance whatever against the highly sophisticated German Army. Fortunately there were those in High Places who realized that this was so. Eventually our Toy Town soldiers went away together with their 'Hoorah Henry' officers. Where they went to, we did not know. It was one of the features of war that people appeared and disappeared, and no one ever asked them whence or whither. The probably went to the Western Desert. I hope they were re-trained before they had to face the cunning 'Desert Fox', General Rommel.

Meanwhile we had the Canadians, who stayed for several years. They were a very different class of men altogether. Their officers were like the bank managers and other officials we were used to. The private soldiers were quiet men from the prairies, who understood the countryside and country ways. In the long years of waiting for the Second Front, they were bored out of their minds with nothing to do. Quite a lot of them came to work on the farm and many close friendships were formed between them and the locals.

Dad Wyatt with Canadian soldiers and cousin John.
(Anti-glider landing barricades behind)

Why did I not serve in the army? The uptake of men, and later women for the war effort very quickly came under strict supervision. Every able-bodied person had to register for some kind of war service. What kind was decided not by the individual but by officialdom. At first all who worked on the land were to stay there. Some of our lads tried to get into the Services, but when it was discovered that they worked on the land, they came back with fleas in their ears and with a few new and rather colourful words added to their vocabularies.

Later, 200,000 young men were taken from the land, among them, my brother Paul. In all honesty I must say that I entered the war as a 'conscientious objector' — a despised 'conshie'. I did not see how a follower of the One who went to a Cross without lifting a finger in His own defence, and who said to His inquisitor, 'If my Kingdom were of this world, then would my servants fight' could bear arms in any circumstances. But when it came to my time to register, the appalling barbarities of the German forces, daily reported in the papers, overcame my spiritual convictions, and I registered as a combatant, if need be.

Meanwhile, the seasons came and went, war or no war. Everything that could be ploughed was ploughed, trenches and barbed wire notwithstanding. Land Girls appeared. You can imagine what the Hacketts thought of them! Some of them were very good workers, and all the extra activities on the farm could not have been carried on without them. Some of them were also very attractive, and friendships were formed which had little to do with either farm work or the war.

But if there is one abiding memory of the war, it is of tiredness. We worked all the daylight hours on the land, and then at night. At first it was Civil Defence duty for me every third night all night. Later, it was Home Guard every seventh night and every Sunday, which had hitherto been a day of rest. When we sat down to meals, we fell asleep into our plates. We fell asleep in the middle of news bulletins on the wireless, we could even have slept on a barbed wire fence at any hour of the day or night. We could, and sometimes did, fall asleep standing up.

I don't know if I am the only member of the Home Guard to take a German prisoner.

On a very dark night in March 1943, a terrible air battle was going on overhead. We had long since given up going to the air raid shelter every time such a thing happened. When it

The Home Guard platoon relaxing after an attack

died down a bit, my father came into my room to see if all was O.K. We went over to the window and pulled aside the blackout curtain. There was a crackling noise in the walnut tree in the garden. I called out 'Who is there?' A voice replied in German. We shot out into the garden and were at the base of the tree as the pilot of a German Bomber clambered down. Only falling into the tree had saved him from the fate of all his companions, who were found dead the next day.

My father and I took him indoors to the farmhouse dining room. He was a young man of about my own age. One of my most vivid war memories is of standing looking at him across the dining room table — he in his Luftwaffe grey with a swastika on his arm; me in my pyjamas and dressing gown. Between us on the table lay his revolver which he had given me in surrender, with a click of his heels. My mother pushed it aside with a tray as she lowered a pot of tea and cups onto the table. Everything about him told me that he was scared out of his wits. Lassie, the farm collie, crept under the table and gave his hand a reassuring lick, before returning to sit beside me. My father was by the door phoning the local Police.

In that moment a feeling of the crass stupidity of war came over me as never before or since. Here were we, two young men facing each other across a table in the middle of the night, bound by a common humanity, yet separated by the lunacy of war — of which the loaded revolver on the polished table was a symbol. He had narrowly escaped death and was in a state of severe shock. I could do nothing about it. To fraternize with the enemy was the unforgivable sin. Soon the house was filled with noisy self-important minor figures from the military world, summoned by my father's phone call and a strange moment, full of human feeling, evaporated.

One of the local Home Guard N.C.O.s expressed the popular mood of the time to me the next day when he said 'You idiot! That man came over here to kill you, and you

Russell and Norman Wyatt harvesting oats in wartime

gave him a cup of tea!'

The war did bring a great sense of fulfilment on the land. Every drop of milk and grain of corn we could produce was desperately needed. The rich coastal loam produced yields which astonished our Canadian helpers, and the whole farm flourished and went from strength to strength in a very satisfying way. There was a great sense of fellowship, whether it was in the sugar beet fields at hoeing time, in the hayfields at tea-time, or coming in from the harvest field with the last load of sheaves at night. In 1940, we would look up from our tasks at the air battles going on overhead, and rush to hear the lunchtime news and learn how many German planes had been shot down that morning. Later in the war we would look up at the serried ranks of bombers going out and wonder if it was the turn of the marshalling yards at Hamm or the Scharnhorst and Gneisnau in Brest Harbour.

The fact that after many months of such bombing, in which a personal friend of mine lost his life, these two pocket battleships came sailing up the Channel one day apparently none the worse for war, is forgotten now. It had a profound effect on us at the time. In the absence of success in other aspects of the war at that time, great prominence was given each day to the bombing campaign both on the wireless and in the newspapers. Were we the dupes of propaganda? From many of the books written about the war, one might suppose that Britain was then inhabited by crowds of 'gung-ho' people waving the Union Jack and cheering every Churchill speech to the echo. Nothing could be further from the truth. The farmers and small business people of the countryside, whose very existence depended on making shrewd assessments of the market situation from day to day, were not easily deceived when it came to assessing the war and our chances of survival.

We did not doubt the success of the Battle of Britain, some of which we had seen with our own eyes as we worked in the fields on those cloudless days in the summer of 1940. All credit to the Flying Officer Kites who won it. But now the whispered question went round — 'Had the Germans really been trying all that hard? With their great technical skill and overwhelming superiority in numbers, could they not have won it? Were we really any more than a petty irritation in their side as they prepared for their real purpose — to destroy forever the Red Empire of Bolshevik Russia?' (I merely report what was said at the time.) Did Hitler have a sneaking regard for our island race on whose Empire the sun never set? Did Hess come to enlist our help in the *drang nach osten*?

When, under the stress of war, people lose faith in what is being told them officially, such a web of fantasy begins to be spun that normally sane folk can lose all touch with reality!

What could not be doubted was that already the mighty panzers were rolling eastwards across the European plain towards the Urals. Country after country had fallen in a matter of days in Spring 1940, before that terrible war machine. Now, a year later, would the same fate befall Russia?

We did not know until later that while we hoed our sugar beet and mowed our hay, thirty million Russians were dying in the ferocious onslaught. We did not know either that as the supply columns of that great army trundled their way eastward along every track and road, train after train was bearing loads of Jews to die in the gas chambers of Auschwitz. (Now, from their air-conditioned offices in Frankfurt or Bonn, the sons and younger brothers of the men who did these deeds, daily lecture us and the Russians on how to run our economies.)

It was all soon to change. The panzers ground to a halt before the forces of Field-Marshall Winter and General Frost. The nightly pounding of Germany by the Lancasters of bomber command began to affect the supply of munitions for the eastern front. But something else was to bring about an astounding effect upon the morale of the country. It was the fresh alert figure of General Montgomery, perky and relaxed.

Wherever 'two or three were gathered together', they gradually stopped talking about Generals Keitel, Von Rundsted and Rommel, and started talking about Monty. The amazing day came when the hitherto silent Church Bells rang out to celebrate the victory at El Alamein. So the Germans were made of flesh and blood like us after all! A mainly British force had beaten a mainly German force in a 'set-piece' battle.

The 'Monty' spirit began to pervade everything, and other senior commanders started to imitate his style. I remember the great uplift of spirits it caused when an 'Order of the Day' appeared on all the Home Guard notice boards in Southern Command, which read, 'ALL ranks will go on route marches: Colonels and corporals and pot-bellied majors, ALL will march without exception'. So the Col. Blimps were 'out' and a new breed of men was in charge. Heads began to be held high once more and spirits rose. As I crouched at night on the beach at Pagham harbour, a member of the Home Guard force deputed to guard the Mulberry Harbour units[1] floating just off shore, and cradling my automatic rifle, I reflected that somewhere along the line I had become a soldier myself.

Even so, none of it seemed as important as what we were doing on the land. At any gathering of farmers the conversation quickly turned from Churchill's latest speech to the best grasses to put into a ley mixture, and the value of sugar beet tops as a feed for milking cows. The war had become an exciting back-drop to our lives, but the real world was on the farm.

*   *   *   *   *

---

[1]   The Mulberry Harbour units were huge hollow barges made of reinforced concrete, which were subsequently towed across the Channel and sunk in a semi-circle to make an artificial harbour to enable heavy equipment for the Normandy invasion to be landed.

Many years after the war, I was leading a party of English young people on a walking holiday in Switzerland. We agreed to join a similar party of German youngsters on an early morning hike to a beauty spot in the mountains for breakfast. As the British and German teenagers jostled and laughed together on the narrow trail, an observant lad asked me about the tears in my eyes. How could I explain my emotions to him? He had never heard the scream of dive-bombers, smelt the stench of blood, urine and cordite, or seen the rows of bodies laid out in neat lines amid the rubble when an air-raid was over. He had probably never once stood by village War Memorials, as I had done on every Remembrance day since the war, listening to long lists of names of the local fallen being read by some worthy, whose quavery voice and misty eyes told of memories of some far-off battlefield — Ypres? Paschendale? Dunkirk? The Anzio Beachhead? Or maybe some blazing oily hell on the northern sea-route to Russia?

I said to him, 'Never mind me, just go off and join the others!' As he went, I wondered if the Norse gods would come again from Valhalla in his generation and exact blood sacrifice from the youth of Europe as they had done twice already in this century — and every other century since the dawn of time.

At breakfast, amid the smell of croissants and coffee, German and English voices blended to sing a Christian hymn — part of our common heritage. For a moment at least, the true Cross had triumphed over the Crooked Cross.

Chapter 12

Max

As the war went on and on, I became more and more resigned to my lot. The idea of studying to be a Missionary or Minister became so seemingly removed from practical reality, that I began to think of being a farmer after all. A farmer needs a wife, of course, and I began to think of that, too. Wise old birds were not lacking with advice, most of it reinforced by illustrations from the farming world. The most useful one was, 'Before you buy a heifer, go and take a look at its mother'.

Anyway, before long I was going out with Max, a lass to whom I have now been married for nearly fifty years. She came from right outside the world of farming. With her lightness and gaiety she brought a whole new and hitherto unthought-of dimension to my rather serious life. The wonderful days of our engagement — of missing the last bus in those days of stringent petrol allowances, and of walking the seven miles home from Chichester in the wee small hours, and many another escapade — are a vivid and happy memory.

To return to the advice I received, her parentage was acceptable in every way not only to me, but also to my parents. Her father was an Anglican parson, and both he and my mother-in-law-to-be were ex-missionaries from Nigeria.

Her family also had to be assured that the family to whom they were entrusting their treasured daughter measured up to their standards. I remember Max's concern that I should pass muster with her Uncle Kelly. He was the acknowledged head of the remaining Maxwell clan, a scientist of no mean order and a member of the Royal Institute. During the First World War he had been Regimental Sergeant Major of the Artists' Rifles.

With great trepidation I awaited his first visit. I thumbed through my farming text books and swotted as many things as I could about which I thought he might ask me. I was told that he did not suffer fools gladly. So I studied my text books and memorized the details of the nutrient requirements of various farm crops and the relative protein and carbohydrate requirements for dairy cows, as opposed to those needed for beef cattle, as well as a mass of other detailed knowledge.

My worst fears seemed to be realized when his first question was as to whether we had any mycetozoa on the farm. I had never heard of mycetozoa. (Was it Latin or Greek for some well-known farm animal?) Great was my relief when I discovered that it was a kind of fungus of decaying timber, and that the worthy uncle's knowledge of, and interest in farming was at the 'cows eat grass' and 'corn grows in fields' level. Once we had found some mycetozoa under a piece of elm bark, we got on famously. One of the greatest compliments I have ever been paid was when he made me his sole trustee and executor.

When all these social inquiries were satisfactorily concluded, a wedding was arranged for 12th January, 1945. There was nothing to be had in the way of new household goods or anything of the sort. I remember phoning Max and saying, 'I've seen a carpet in a shop in Bognor for £18'. The fact that it was old and worn with a hole in one corner and of a nondescript colour did not matter. It was a carpet, and we rushed in and bought it. The same went for two ancient and uncomfortable armchairs. It is impossible to convey to folk born since the war, the state that the country was in at that time.

But a great sadness awaited us. On Boxing Day, 1944 our family went for the traditional Shoot with friends and neighbours. My father slipped in the snow and his hernia came out and could not be reduced. He was soon in a private ward in the Royal West Sussex Hospital — the very place where Max was doing her nursing training. A question mark then came over the date of the wedding. In the end, it was decided that we could not cancel at short notice the arrangements which had been made with such difficulty. We reconciled ourselves to the fact that my father would not be there. He was very fond of Max, and very happy about it all. I went to see him on the morning of the wedding day as he lay in hospital, not allowed to move.

So it was that on one of the coldest days I ever remember, Max and I were married in Holy Trinity Church, Hove, where her father, the Rev'd Lowry Maxwell, was the Vicar. My brother Russell was my best man (in the absence of Paul in Germany). We went to our honeymoon at Eastbourne, which was covered by thick snow. There were five aprons of barbed wire sealing off the beach, almost every shop window was boarded up because of bomb blast, and nearly every road had a bomb hole in it. There was no central heating in the hotel, and a bunch of elderly crones formed a circle so that no outsider could get anywhere near the miserable fire that glowed in the grate. It was not long before we fled to the comfort of a roaring home fire, piled with logs from the farm.

We had hardly got back from our honeymoon when a phone call from Chichester informed us that my father had had a relapse. A day later, while I was alone with him, he died. It totally changed our world. The end of the war, when it came four months later, was as nothing to me compared with the death of my father. However it settled one thing for me for the foreseeable future. With Paul in Germany, Russell on the point of leaving school, and my two younger sisters still at school, there could be no doubt that it was my duty to run the family business. There was now no thought of my being anything but a farmer.

Chapter 13

Last Days at Walberton

With my father gone, and the war which had threatened all my life finished, nothing was ever the same again at Walberton. After the brief rejoicing at Victory came the grim realization of what it had cost us all. We were victorious, but all of Europe, as well as our own great cities, lay in ruins. Food and petrol rations went down in quantity and up in price.

The 1945 General Election which swept Labour to power with a huge majority was greeted by stunned disbelief in rural Sussex. No wartime reverse had ever cast such a gloom over us. Churchill was gone, and so was Roosevelt. It seemed to us that pygmies now sat in the seats vacated by giants. Uncle Joe Stalin smiled contentedly and tightened his grip on half Europe.

The dismantling of the British Empire now began and the grey hand of Socialism took all the life and colour out of the national scene. One by one, Bill Sergeant's prophecies were fulfilled. Men who had been great heroes in uniform found that in 'civvy street' they were barely employable.

Up-and-coming young farmers started looking abroad for farms, and there were not a few who whispered that the old country was finished. A number of my contemporaries and friends emigrated.

It was in this atmosphere that I leapt at the opportunity to go abroad and see for myself that greener grass that many said was there on the other side of the fence. Russell was engaged to be married and wanted me to go out to Northern Rhodesia[1]

---

[1] Now Zambia

to see his farm and be Best Man at his wedding. With my mother, I presented myself at the Nissen-Huts-in-a-field which was all Heathrow then consisted of, and flew off on the three-day journey to Central Africa. I had never before been out of England. Now in a few hours I saw Paris, Rome, Malta, Cairo, Khartoum, Nairobi, and flew on over the vast expanses of sub-Sahara Africa. It was a bewildering experience. It was very liberating to be out of the atmosphere of war and its aftermath. All looked fresh and lovely, compared with the drabness of an England in which everything was either worn out or destroyed by war.

The wedding over, I set about the secret part of my mission, and boarded a train for the week-long journey to Salisbury in Southern Rhodesia, to look for a farm to buy. The first morning in Meikles Hotel in Salisbury I was reading my Bible in bed when the Spirit spoke to me in a way I have seldom experienced. The morning portion contained the words, 'Arise ye and depart, for this is not your rest. Because it is polluted it will destroy you even with a sore destruction'. I felt I had been pole-axed. I left that country as soon as I could make the arrangements.

A family of my close friends did go there. Their only son, the same age as mine, died in that futile war, the last of the Colonial wars fought by men of British stock. It was all to no avail. Through international pressure, victory came to the extremists, and a regime combining the black and white races was swept away. Many of the wealth creators left in despair to start life again elsewhere. The result has been that a beautiful country, rich in natural resources, which was once the grain bin for all the countries around about, now shamelessly holds up its begging bowl with all the other African states that once prospered under the flag of Empire.

I came back to England and to the farm with one thing settled. We would not emigrate. But I was not happy with my lot, and neither was Max. The old niggle came back. I had never wanted to be a farmer, but too much time had now gone by to go to College. Besides there was my mother who partly depended on me, and also Max's parents, who by this time had come to live with us. On top of all this, we had two small children, Richard and Felicity.

The farms were not mine, nor was the money that was invested in them, except for the one small farm at Bognor which my father had passed to me before he died. My two brothers had to be considered, and my younger sisters had not completed their education. All had been left in Trust for the six of us, but the income was to go to my mother for the rest of her life.

Norman with Max at Pigeon House Farm, in the late 1940s

There were long meetings of my father's executors. In the end the two smaller farms were disposed of, I became my mother's tenant on the farm at Walberton, and Paul moved to a farm at Slindon, somewhat larger than the family farm. Money was sent out to Northern Rhodesia to fund Russell's enterprises there.

The settlement was that each of the six of us received £1,000 as a gift from the estate. Paul, Russell and I were each given a loan of £4,000. (In those days a family car cost about £400, whereas today a similar car would cost £12,000. On that basis, each £1,000 would be £30,000 today.) The interest on these loans provided my mother with an income. As time went on, Paul and I had to increase the rate of our interest payments to unrealistic levels to maintain my mother.

This arrangement drained much money from the family farm, but the banks were helpful. However, we were all in a financial straight-jacket together. The pre-war philosophy of hard work and thrift still survived and the days were yet to come when banks lent freely and foolishly to all and sundry. How grateful I am now that they refused to finance some of my wilder schemes!

Meanwhile, the underlying discontent would not go away. Were we going to spend our lives doing what we did not really want to do? This fire did not burn all the time, and we had much joy in our two little ones, and it was super that Granny and Grandpa Maxwell could also share their baby days. As pioneer missionaries, they had been robbed of this privilege with their own children.

Grandpa became popular with Old Tommy and the Hacketts. He patiently visited the casual labourers who came to hoe the sugar beet fields, and for a time formed a valuable link between the Church and Chapel by giving joint Bible Teaching. Alas, this was ended by an edict from some small-minded Church official. The saintly Bishop Bell with his wide ecumenical sympathies and his respect for Grandpa himself would have been horrified by this ruling. Grandpa daily prayed Christ's prayer for the unity of all God's people, but that unity was set back in our village for several more years by an exclusivism which this time came from the Established Church.

Max and Felicity

A few years later, the first Billy Graham Crusade took place, and this was the catalyst we had been waiting for. Max and I became involved not only with the Harringay Campaign, but with its many ripples in our own area. Joint prayer meetings were organised, and I was even invited to go with the local Vicar, Mr. Lunn, to a meeting chaired by Bishop Bell, at his palace in Chichester. The Vicar and I became fast friends. People started praying together who hitherto had hardly been on speaking terms. And in us the fire burned.

We decided at last that we were not going to spend the rest of our lives in farming. If I could not train and become a Minister, then at least we must find some way of life that would enable us both to find fulfilment. Spurred on by the example of some older friends, but to the dismay of our farming acquaintances, we decided to get out of farming and purchase a country house and start a home for the elderly. Max would find an outlet for her skills in this, and I would be more free to pursue my growing spiritual ministry. Ideas were one thing, but how to do it was another. The midnight oil was burnt, working out one scheme after another. Eventually we decided to do just what our Lord told his disciples to do: 'Ask and ye shall receive, seek and ye shall find, knock and the door shall be opened unto you'. There was a business side to our decision.

As I rode the combine harvester in summer, with my little son strapped to the machine beside me, or as I strode through the wet kale in winter to move the electric fence for the cows, I reflected on the changing pattern of farming. I was not my father's son for nothing. Spiralling costs, especially wage costs, were spelling the death knell of the old labour-intensive mixed farms such as ours. One must change, or go out of business. The new machines and labour-saving buildings needed scale to justify the outlay. One could not have scale on a medium-sized farm, without specialising.

Many men were doing it already, including Paul, who was

concentrating his whole enterprise on the dairy herd. I was not willing to do this. Like Russell, Paul was a skilled cattle breeder and geneticist, whereas I was not. While I had been studying theology, they had been studying the scientific aspects of farming.

On the other hand, my farm was not large enough or suitable in other ways to be a viable arable enterprise. Besides, I liked the variety of the old mixed farming system and the involvement it brought with people. Grandpa Wyatt had failed in farming business because he was a romantic, and would not take hard business decisions. I had his example to warn me. Many farmers had not yet woken up to what was happening. Some in our acreage bracket quietly went down the drain, wondering to the last what they were doing wrong. But for us there was still time to get out, retaining our capital for more fruitful ventures. Within a few weeks of deciding to 'Ask, Seek and Knock', we had arranged to dispose of our farming interests.

Such a radical change in our way of life had its traumatic side. The milking machine which my father installed in 1927 and which had run every morning and every evening for thirty years, including the war years, ceased to run. The herd of cattle and all those machines which the incoming farmer did not want were sold. With the cattle gone, a silence settled upon the farm which had hitherto been a hive of noisy activity. For the first time in my life, we ordered milk which was delivered in bottles to our door, in the weeks before we vacated the farmhouse. It was this simple thing more than any other that brought home to me the enormity of what we had done.

Three months later, on Lady Day, 1958, we moved to a Victorian mansion in the village of Rake on the very western edge of Sussex, made famous by Kipling's description of Sussex as 'that land which lies twixt Rake and Rye'. It had beautiful park-like grounds extending to thirty-five acres. We had purchased it for £1,000 more than my father had paid for the farm twenty-three years previously. We did so amid dire predictions of disaster from many of our friends.

Although we did not do it for business reasons only, we had carefully researched our new market. It proved to be the best business move we ever made. So, like Jacob with his flocks and herds, we went with our old folks, Granny and Grandpa Maxwell, our two children, and our faithful old dogs to start a new life. And like Abraham, there was a sense in which we went out 'not knowing whither we went'. We certainly did not know all the trials and all the glories which awaited us in our new life, on that blustery March day in 1958, but we were excited. I had lived just half the allotted span when we sold the farm. It took me a few years to adjust and then for me, as for many another, life began at forty.

Chapter 14

Reflections

As I look back on my life at Walberton over an expanse of nearly forty years, it is the failure of my school years that still troubles me most and about which I debate frequently with myself. It has been a constant handicap to me. This was compounded by the fact that the advent of war deprived me of the chance to go to college. I am highly embarrassed every time I have to fill in a form which requires me to state my educational qualifications, for I left school with none.

I soon realized that this simply would not do, and set about educating myself. I had no one to guide me. I tried to master such tomes as Fream's 'Elements of Agriculture' and Prof. Hagedoorn's great standard work on genetics among a host of lesser works on agriculture. But it was on the Biblical and social side of things that I read most widely and deeply. My bedroom was filled with several ten-volume Bible Commentaries; that the ones I bought were cheaply available in second-hand shops should have alerted me to the fact that they might not be the best, but it did not. However, *Uncle Tom's Cabin* and Bunyan's *The Pilgrim's Progress* first opened for me a window on to the great religious and social struggles of the seventeenth, eighteenth and nineteenth centuries. Such characters as Simon Legree the Slave Trade and Mr. Worldywiseman became as familiar to me as Bill Sergeant and old Tommy Dowling.

Above all, I soaked myself in the Bible itself until, like Grandpa Wyatt and my father, I lived in 'the communion of saints'. Years later, someone with whom I was on holiday said to me, 'You talk as if you know Abraham and Joseph and all these people personally'. Well, I do know them! I got to know them in those days, and their lives, with their strengths and weaknesses, have helped me in many a tight corner since. Each weekend, with local preaching and Bible Class leading to do, provided the necessary discipline to make sure that I kept up with my studies.

A number of things puzzled me, and I had no tutor to whom to turn. Why, for example, had history handed the accolade to the Wesley Brothers with their wishy-washy Arminianism, when it was George Whitefield, with his strong Calvinistic emphasis on the Grace of God, who seemingly made the greater impact in their day? Also at that time, I firmly held the Baptist belief that Christian baptism should only be given to adults who can give a clear confession of faith. Why was it, I wondered, that none of the reformers, none of the ancient fathers, and none of the leaders of the Evangelical Revival held this view? Indeed some of the reformers were most vociferous in advocating that baptism should not be withheld from babies because of the unworthiness of their parents.

I was yet to come fully to Whitefield's realization: that important as faith and obedience are, it is God Who is the prime mover in all matters of Salvation, and that He reaches out in Grace to us and waits with infinite patience for our feeble faith. And when faith and understanding are lacking, He still persists. As St. Paul wrote to his son Timothy, 'If we believe not, yet He abideth faithful — He cannot deny Himself'. When the time came and the 'fiery cloudy pillar'[1] moved on for me out of Nonconformity and back into the Established Church, which both of my grandfathers had deserted for the Open Brethren, baptism was no problem for me, as it has been

---

[1] The second verse of the hymn 'Guide me, O Thou great Jehovah' by W. Williams has the lines :
  'Let the fiery, cloudy pillar
  Lead me all my journey through'.

for the very many who have made this pilgrimage before me.

It was in the early mornings and the long winter evenings at Walberton that I taught myself the disciplines of study and meditation, which still form a major part of my life.

I did not pursue my inner pilgrimage alone. Chapel and the Open Assembly of Brethren in Littlehampton played a large part in it. New influences were beginning to be felt, a foretaste of the Charismatic revival yet to come. Among these were the teachings of the Ruanda Revival people. At first we were taken by their holiness and what seemed the simple sincerity of their message: 'We must be honest before God and before one another. We must confess our faults, and be open to others challenging us for faults we do not recognize in ourselves'. But it was not long before we realized that the way some of them practised it was opening the door, on the one hand, to an unhealthy introspection, and a downgrading of the Gospel which proclaimed 'their sins and their iniquities will I remember no more'. (Here were we, racking our brains to remember what God had forgotten); and on the other hand, it was leading to a kind of upside down 'one-upmanship': Who was the biggest sinner, and who the most honest confessor of his faults? We turned away from it to the honest to God simple faith of our fathers.

All this was reinforced when the Charismatic revival eventually burst upon the Church. As well as a great new release of spiritual life, a kind of 'two-tier' Christianity seemed to be proclaimed for a while. Had you had 'IT' or had you not? To the initiated, 'IT' was baptism in the Holy Spirit. But for many excited young people, I fear that it was the supernatural gift of speaking in tongues that was the attraction. It was then that my Walberton Chapel experience of the Ruanda Revival Fellowship stood me in good stead. It had taught me that an over-emphasis on one aspect of the many-sided truth of God can be divisive and even destructive. By that time, I was British General Secretary of the Africa

Evangelical Fellowship, a Missionary Society working in fourteen countries in southern Africa.

I soon found myself playing 'piggy-in-the-middle' between an almost entirely Charismatic missionary force and an almost entirely anti-Charismatic Home Council. To the missionaries I would say, 'Thank God for the experience he has given you. But please do not make a doctrine out of it to which everyone else has to subscribe'. To the Council I would say, 'The experience they have had is scriptural and valid, and you deny it at your peril'.

I thank God for what the Charismatic revival has done for many folk, and for the influence for good it has had on the whole Church. Alas that some sections have felt it necessary to leave their established denominations for uncharted waters. I tremble for them. The long history of the Church is full of the disasters caused when Christians forsake the discipline of a balanced spiritual order to 'major' on one aspect of God's truth. The history of the Exclusive Brethren alone should be enough to warn the spiritually sensitive of the folly of this course of action. Also, try as I may, I can never finish a book by any of the well-known Charismatic gurus. Their writings seem slight and inconsequential to me, compared with those of the great spiritual giants of this, and former generations.

But the deepest and most fundamental legacy of Walberton is the faith that I learned from my father and Grandpa Wyatt, from Mr. Henry Humphrey and a horde of other worthies. The Christ who walked with me daily has grown into a stronger Presence as the years go by.

Consequently, when the Bishop of Guildford, who did not know me then, asked me in an interview prior to Ordination: 'Do the things that the Bishop of Durham says upset your faith?', I was so astonished that my first impulse was to laugh. Had I not been talking to the Risen Lord in my car a few minutes before? The Bishop of Durham indeed! I nearly answered facetiously in the words of Michael Flanders about the former Bishop of Woolwich — 'He doesn't really exist you know. He's just an idea in the mind of God'.

I am writing here of David Jenkins, Bishop of Durham and the late John Robinson, former Bishop of Woolwich, as popularly perceived. The media has done a great disservice to both men and to the general public by what amounts almost to a distortion of their beliefs. No one believed in God more profoundly than John Robinson, and this was shown in the way he took his long last illness. Yet he was widely represented as a trendy Bishop who didn't believe in God when his book *Honest to God* was published. I can personally testify to the strength of this misconception about him. With Max, I went to see 'At the Drop of a Hat' during the 'sixties. Michael Flanders' quip: 'He doesn't really exist you know. He's just an idea in the mind of God', brought the loudest and longest laugh of the evening.

In the same way many people think that David Jenkins doesn't believe in the resurrection of Jesus. Here is what he wrote himself in one of his books. 'Risen He (Jesus) was and risen He is. There is a fact here which is a fact of the world and a fact for the world. Jesus was dead and God raised Him up'.

However, neither man can entirely escape blame for what has happened to his pronouncements. They write and speak in the provocative manner of the classroom and lecture hall. This greatly distresses many of the 'Faithful' who expect their Bishops to be shepherds. It also greatly delights those who have a vested interest in presenting the modern Church as apostate. The initial fury with which Archbishop Ramsey greeted John Robinson's 'Honest to God' was surely in the truer tradition of those charged with the awesome task of shepherding the flock of God.

Many a great saint throughout the long history of the

Church has wrestled his way towards faith through the kind of problem which troubles Dr. Jenkins, including St. Augustine himself. A faith which claims to know all the answers is not a Biblical faith. Even our Lord Jesus himself cried out 'My God, My God why . . .?' a few moments before He yielded up His Spirit. But His last words were, 'Father, into Thy hands I commit my spirit'. So in spite of all, there was a God to whom to address the question, and a Father to trust when all else fails.

As I sat there before the Bishop of Guildford, with his question as to whether the Bishop of Durham had upset my faith, hanging in the air between us, all these thoughts rushed through my mind. This was obviously the key question of the interview. How could I respond? I groped for words. Eventually, I managed to say, 'I could more easily doubt that I am sitting here talking to you, than I could doubt the existence and the love of God'.

It came over more strongly than I intended, and the Bishop eyed me narrowly. That he appointed a stern Anglo-Catholic Priest to train me in Anglican ways, I blame on this outburst of mine. This pernickety little man was in the spiritual succession of Dons who had had the Wesley brothers thrown out of Oxford for showing 'enthusiasm in religion'. The least sign of enthusiasm on my part, and he was down on me like a ton of bricks. But I learnt a lot from him. I also learnt a lot from the whole episode. I now weigh my words more carefully when talking to Bishops and other hierarchs of the Church.

It was also at Walberton that I learned to trust God's guidance. It so puzzles the young, and it puzzled me for years. Why had the Lord so dealt with me over my desire to be a Minister and a Missionary? Should I have gone ahead against my parents' advice at the beginning of the war, and bludgeoned my way into training? Should I have ditched the farm the moment war ended, and gone ahead then? I learnt, slowly and falteringly at first, to discern when the moment was right to move, and when it was right to stay. It is the story of the pillar of cloud by day and the pillar of fire by night that has helped me 'all my journey through' as it did William Williams, the great Welsh hymn writer. When things are settled and all is as clear as day, the eye must always be upon that cloud of mystery in which God dwells. Is it stationary, or is it slowly moving on? It is different when the chips are down, and the darkness of the world threatens to engulf. Then 'the fiery, cloudy pillar' lights up the way, and one walks surely and confidently.

Great, too, are the moments when that *'shekinah'* that shone in the ancient Sanctuary comes from the heavens to alight upon the Eucharist, or to shine from the face of a Henry Humphrey or some other modern Moses, as he sets forth the Word of God. For me, as I write, that pillar of cloud is moving off again, and I must follow or lose touch. As a great first century pilgrim wrote, 'Here we have no continuing city, but we seek one to come'.

Chapter 15

Threshing Days: A Postscript

The pillar of cloud by day and the pillar of fire by night are only visible to the eye of faith. In the Bible story, I am sure they were not seen by the Egyptians, but only by the Pilgrim People of God as they set out for the Promised Land. Had the Egyptians been told about them, they would doubtless have dismissed them at once as figments of pious imagination.

Yet, meaningless as they may be to the worldly mind, these twin symbols of God's guidance are not some magical display far removed from practical reality. The Holy Spirit Who guides the People of God does so by causing them to see life from a spiritual standpoint. They thus come to conclusions which cannot be arrived at merely by a process of natural reasoning. Natural reasoning there must be, of course, but over and above it ever stands the fiery, cloudy pillar.

As I now conclude this account of my early life, it is, strangely, something as down to earth as the evolution of corn-threshing which best illustrates how this powerful spiritual phenomenon acted in my case.

Before the advent of combine harvesters, no farm of our size boasted its own threshing tackle. For one thing, the tractors we had then were not powerful enough to drive a threshing machine, let alone when combined with an elevator or a baler. These latter were an essential part of the process. So we relied on the steam-driven tackle provided by contractors.

In our area, the most popular contractor was James Lear Penfold, of Barnham. The elderly founder of this large contracting firm had left his empire of steam wagons, lorries, and gravel pits to his sons. He himself concentrated on his one

magnificently maintained set of threshing tackle. I do not exaggerate when I use the word magnificent. Mr. Penfold was a perfectionist in all he had and did. He drove about in his spotless Bentley and generally behaved like the superior being he considered himself to be.

The family of men Mr. Penfold employed to run his threshing business were of the same ilk as the Hacketts. 'Nobby' North, an aged tyrant, presided over his many sons and tended his beloved steam engine with single-minded taciturnity. Each afternoon, as the great fly wheel spun, the piston hissed its release of steam at every revolution, the main drive belt gently flapped and the drum hummed sweetly, Nobby would polish each of the many brass plates and bands on the great engine until you could see to comb your hair in them.

It was James Penfold's habit to allow each of his many customers one day's threshing during or immediately after harvest. He gave little warning, or none. He would then return, entirely at his own convenience, at some later time in the winter and give a week's threshing. If that did not suffice to thresh all the ricks of the previous year's harvest, he would return for a third time. Although we paid very handsomely for his services, he always treated us like peasants who ought to be grateful for the attention of one so lordly and so able. My father put up with this, as he did all his other customers, because no other contractor in the area could touch him with a barge pole when it came to efficiency. No grain of corn remained on straw which had been over his drum. All went into the sack — and cleanly, too.

Threshing gang, including the Hackett brothers

Threshing days were great days in the life of the farm. At the first sound of the iron-wheeled steam engine coming up the lane to the farm with all the clatter of the long tail of machines which came swaying in its wake, the heart missed a beat and then did not return to normal until the last whiff of choking coal smoke from the retreating dinosaur had died away a day, or maybe a week later.

At the first sight of Nobby North, erect and grimy at the controls of the steam engine, with his eldest son beside him, everything on the farm became a frenzy of activity. Sacks had to be collected from the corn merchant, coal and water delivered to the threshing site, and tasks allocated to the hoard of workers who would attend to the needs of the devouring monster in our midst. The poor old cows came in where they could, for no one really had time to think much about them and their needs during threshing days.

The Hacketts and the Norths would eye each other sourly, and never by word or gesture give any hint of the profound respect they felt for each other. For it was a known thing that no other gang of men for miles around could keep the sheaves flowing in a steady stream to the drum for hour after hour like the Hacketts could. And it was equally well known that from the first almighty 'Chuff' of the steam engine, as Nobby let in the control in the murky early morning light of a winter's day until knocking-off time, no other threshing gang in the whole area could keep the steady hum of the drum going as did the Norths. Their machinery never broke down, the engine never lost steam, nor did the belts come off from careless alignment of the string of machines. The feeding was so smooth that the drum never choked and snapped the belts. BUT there were fourteen men and women doing what does not need to be done at all today. What would our food cost if they were all paid today's wage rates?

Like all the farming routines of those days, threshing had its own lore and its own language. Up on top of the drum stood two of Nobby's sons, one a bond-cutter and one a feeder. Yet another did the sacking off, and then there were the four landgirls allocated to the threshing tackle. They did the racketings and helped on the straw rick, which was always presided over by Tommy Dowling. Several of us kept the hungry and thirsty monster supplied with coal and water, and carted away the wheat, oats or barley to the barns at the farm buildings. At the end of the day, we could all have gone straight on to a stage as black and white minstrels, especially the landgirls, who came heavily made-up in the morning. This provided a marvellous base for the coal smuts, and racketing dust . . . But they were great days, and the smell of a steam engine always makes my heart beat faster to this day.

Gradually it all changed. Balers became more sophisticated and took the place of the early crude ones, or the even earlier elevators, which sent great waves of loose straw billowing on to the rick, requiring considerable skill and physical strength to build into any kind of thatchable shape. Tommy Dowling was an expert at this, and even found time to pass cheeky remarks at any one who came within range. One chilly winter's day, when the engine smoke blew level from the funnel and the rooks made baskets in the sky, my father came walking down to see how we were getting on. He had been quite ill. Tommy looked over the side of the rick and shouted out, 'Don't you get comin' down 'ere standin' about, or they old bronchalows will get 'old of 'ee!' Tommy responded to the general air of excitement caused by threshing as much as any of us.

I am both sad and glad that those days have gone. I shall never forget two of the Hackett brothers sitting on a stile years later, watching as I combined a field in less time than the initial cutting with a binder would have taken. In that one operation not only was the threshing taken care of, but the binding, the stooking, the carting, the ricking, and the thatching. As I drew the machine up by the gate to greet them in the fading light of the summer evening, they were very excited. I don't think it dawned on them then that they were attending the funeral of many of their skills, and of a way of life that had continued with very little change for many generations. But they were old men, and soon to go the way of all flesh themselves. Maybe it was some kind of generosity of spirit, a nod to the new age, that made them so excited.

I did not share their excitement, but rather a sense of guilt. I knew that I was fast becoming the agent of things that were going to destroy their way of life, as well as putting the wonderful world of my youth forever beyond my own grasp. On my shoulders rode the twin demons of Improving Technology and Financial Pressure. Had I had Grandpa Wyatt's incandescent spirituality, I would have exorcised them at once and to hell with the consequences. But there was a little too much of Grandpa Norman in me for that. I did rid myself of them in the end, however, by leaving farming altogether. By great good fortune, and by the good hand of my God upon me, I did this with my capital and my health intact but — as Wellington said of the battle of Waterloo — 'it was a damn close-run thing'. However, like the nights of the Kerry Dancing in the old song, so with the Threshing Days. 'Just to think of them, just to dream of them fills my heart with tears . . . they are gone, alas, like my youth — too soon'.

On that autumn day described in the beginning of this book, Russell, Max and I turned away in silence from our parents' and grandparents' graves. The memorial words on my father's tomb, from the Letter to the Hebrews, were going over and over in my mind: *'Ye have in heaven a better and an enduring substance'*. Silently we walked across the meadow where we used to smell 'the milky breath of cattle laid at ease'[1] on summer evenings long ago. We averted our eyes from the rash of modern houses which scarred the field between the farmstead and the farmhouse. We turned to look back across the fields to where copses once gave cover to pheasants and where once we made our childish bows and arrows. Some of the copses were gone, as were many of the hedges with their stately solitary trees. As we neared the farm buildings we could see that even the ancient flint Pigeon House had been 'restored'. We ourselves had also changed. Only the Saxon Church was just as we had always remembered it.

---

[1]   from 'Sussex Cattle' by Rudyard Kipling